Making The Grade:
Academic Libraries And Student Success

Edited by
Maurie Caitlin Kelly and Andrea Kross

Association of College and Research Libraries
A division of the American Library Association
Chicago, 2002

The paper used in this publication meets the minimum requirements of American National Standard for Information Sciences–Permanence of Paper for Printed Library Materials, ANSI Z39.48—1992.∞

Library of Congress Cataloging-in-Publication Data

Making the grade : academic libraries and student success / edited by Maurie Caitlin Kelly and Andrea Kross.
    p. cm.
Includes bibliographical references.
  ISBN 0-8389-8177-1 (alk. paper)
  1. Academic libraries—Aims and objectives—United States. 2. Library orientation for college students—United States. 3. Academic libraries—United States—Relations with faculty and curriculum. 4. Libraries and students—United States. I. Kelly, Maurie Caitlin. II. Kross, Andrea.
  Z675.U5 M326 2002
  027.7'0973—dc21
                          2001007575

05 04 03   5 4 3 2

Table Of Contents

Introduction

Maurie Caitlin Kelly

There is an old African proverb, "It takes a whole village to educate a child." Apply this to a university setting and it becomes, "it takes a whole university to educate a student." This statement emphasizes the partnership, vision, and mission of all universities in educating and retaining students. It also affirms the partnership among the university community that must be present to make every student's goal of receiving a degree a reality. It clearly reflects the responsibility that every member of the university community has to its student population. It is simply why we are here.

Student success, which can be defined as a student completing a program of study, is the result of an effective program or approach to student retention and serves as a reflection of the successful partnership between the university and the student. Every member of the university community has a role and responsibility in retaining students and assisting students to reach their goal. Every member of the university community also has a responsibility to develop and provide services and support.

It is important not to view academic retention in qualitative terms alone, such as graduation rate and GPA, but to also look beyond the most common definitions to embrace a more comprehensive view by examining the types of academic support, services, and outreach that play an important role in student success. For many students, issues affecting their success include course availability and support, availability of academic support for difficult courses in the form of tutors or mentors, more effective teaching assistants, increased access to academic advisors and guidance, and intervention programs for students at risk. They also include a positive freshman experience and introduction to the university, the successful development of research skills, positive interactions with the university community, and access to computing services and information resources. The library is, by far, one of the most important partners in this process.

Libraries, by function, are an integral part of the lives of students at a university. They are often the technology base of the campus—providing computing resources such as labs, Internet access, and computing infrastructure. Libraries are also a place to gather and study in groups, a place where necessary resources are provided and research assistance can be easily obtained. In recent years, the role of the library has expanded, in many ways as a result of new technologies.

Technology has caused the redefinition of roles and responsibilities for libraries in an academic environment, and within those libraries, the roles of academic librarians have undergone fundamental changes. The environment, resources, and techniques have changed, and have added significant demands in terms of expertise, technical knowledge, and skills. These demands have increased by requiring that both traditional resources and services be provided while asking that libraries and librarians remain on the cutting edge of technology through the development of new services and the acquisition of state of the art computing resources. All of these elements have an impact on the experiences students have in their academic library and, in turn, an impact on their academic success.

As the success and retention of students has grown in importance, so have the responsibilities of many academic libraries in playing a more active role in this retention.

In order to address the issue of student success, libraries have fostered a greater awareness of student issues, developed additional outreach services such as freshman and required courses and programs, examined alternative approaches to diversity, and collaborated more often and more effectively with faculty outside the library.

This book endeavors to provide insight into these new demands and responsibilities, while providing practical examples of programs, policies, and projects. By taking the lead in developing these new services, these librarians have made a definite impact on the success of students in their colleges and universities and have helped those students 'make the grade'.

Library Mission Statements:
Effective Tools for Change

Andrea Kross

Introduction

Mission statements have a bad reputation. Many people think of them as mere words on paper, with messages so general and sappy that they are meaningless and could apply to any firm, so obvious that they hardly need mentioning, or full of lies and false political correctness, purporting that the organization values things that employees and customers know it does not, with the end result that no one will pay any attention to them anyway (Wright 1996; Hardesty, Hastreiter, and Henderson 1985; Albrecht 1994). The literature indicates that these kinds of mission statements occur with alarming frequency. Yet, the problem in these cases is not with the mission statement per se but, rather, with the organization not taking the time to either write an effective mission statement, or not bothering to implement its mission statement to the fullest extent.

It is very easy to find samples of mission statements on the Internet or in books such as those written by Hardesty, Hastreiter, and Henderson (1985), and Graham and Havlick (1994). Research on 120 academic libraries found that "rather than having derived these [mission] statements from institutional uniqueness, they typically adopted language from professional associations such as the American Library Association" (Bangert 1997, 94). But does this cookie-cutter method of creating a mission statement give the desired results? Those who feel that the library's mission is self-evident might be surprised to find that it is more difficult to articulate than they thought, and if the library's mission is not very clear to librarians, it is even less clear to the college/university administration and classroom faculty (Hardesty, Hastreiter, and Henderson 1988).

The Role of the Mission Statement

At the most basic level, the mission statement explains why the organization exists. More specifically, it is a description of the organization's purpose, unique services and/or products, philosophy, values, aspirations, and desired image. Mission statements have been called promises to patrons (DeCandido 1995). Campbell and Yeung (1990) contend that the mission statement has four components: the purpose, describing what business the organization is in and why; the strategy, which describes how the organization's uniqueness will help it to achieve the purpose; behavior standards, expectations of how employees should behave on a day-to-day basis; and values, the moral and ethical convictions of the organization's employees, including upper management. It sets the tone for how things are and will be done at that organization (Brophy 1991) and describes the organization's responsibilities toward stakeholders, ensuring that their interests are not ignored (Campbell and Yeung 1990; Bart 1997b). Some say the mission statement should describe what the organization plans to do in the future, and how (Morrisey 1988); others assert that the mission statement should only include what the organization is in the present (Campbell and Yeung 1990).

The mission statement is often couched in broad terms, indicating a general direction while allowing for a wide range of specific actions and goals. As such, it is an essential component in strategic planning, where it provides the framework for a strategic management plan that culminates in specific goals and objectives. It is often the only part of the strategic plan that is publicized (Cochran, David, and Gibson 1985), and it can be very effective as a unifying force to keep everyone focused on the same purpose. However, if the strategic plan is not implemented, there may be dissatisfaction with the mission statement, which is not always the fault of the mission statement but, rather, a failure to follow through on the part of management (Baetz and Bart 1996). If the mission statement is not an accurate reflection of a particular organization, it cannot be a strong foundation for that organization's strategic plans, goals, and policies (Cochran, David, and Gibson 1985).

There are other practical reasons to have a mission statement. For libraries in particular, either a mission statement or a set of objectives and goals can be a requirement of regional accreditation agencies (Hardesty, Hastreiter, and Henderson 1988; Bangert 1997). In view of increasing competition for funding and resources, publicizing a mission statement can be a method of gaining the support and understanding of the library's parent institution, faculty, staff, administration, board members, patrons, alumni, the community, government, and other key stakeholders such as suppliers and financial backers or those who are responsible for allocating funds to the library. More generally, the mission statement provides a sense of direction, a clear purpose, and a point of reference for every decision to be made by acting as a reminder of why the organization exists. One area of decision-making where it can be especially helpful is resource allocation. If worded carefully, mission statements are also useful in motivating and inspiring employees (Cochran, David, and Gibson 1985), clarifying each employee's job and how it contributes to the bigger picture (Porter 1997; Baetz and Bart 1996; Woods 1988). They provide standards of behavior that all employees, including senior management, are expected to abide by; for senior managers, they are also a guide to ensure consistent leadership styles (Baetz and Bart 1996). Mission statements articulate the culture of the organization, which determines how employees will instinctively react when faced with a new or difficult situation; management in organizations with a strong culture will know how their employees will react and those in a weak culture will not (Calfee 1993; Wright 1996). Campbell and Yeung (1990) note that defining a culture in a mission statement will not automatically make it so; rather, the mission statement should reflect the culture that already exists, but by doing so, it ensures that everyone is clear on what is expected (Campbell and Yeung 1990; Woods 1988). The mission statement is a way for the organization to describe its values; when those values match with the employees' individual values, the result is dedicated, loyal employees who feel their work is worthwhile and who require less supervision (Campbell and Yeung 1990). Studies of nonprofit organizations reveal that having a clear mission statement and accompanying goals is critical to being successful (Stone 1996). Properly formulated, the mission statement can be an aid to measure and evaluate progress (Hardesty, Hastreiter, and Henderson 1988). Finally, the process of writing the statement, thinking about all the issues involved, and defining the organization's purpose is a very valuable exercise in itself, as important as the result of that effort.

Various studies have examined how mission statements are actually used. A survey of academic libraries revealed that mission statements were used to relate the library's purpose and objectives to those of faculty, administration, and students; to improve the services of the library; and to assist in collection development. Resource allocation, strangely, did not rank high (Hardesty, Hastreiter, and Henderson 1985). In surveys of businesses, this was also the case (Baetz and Bart 1996), which the researchers saw as a missed opportunity. Vardi, Wiener, and Popper (1989) examined the effect of the mission statement on employee behavior by studying two companies in Israel that were nearly identical except for their mission statements: One statement was more in line with the values held by Israeli society, namely defense, survival, and national security; the other mission statement did not include any reference to these values. They found that employees of the company with the value-loaded mission statement "exhibit[ed] higher organizational identification, pride and willingness for self-sacrifice" than employees of the other company (31). Bart (1996) found that specifying an innovative behavior in the mission statement resulted in a higher incidence of that behavior.

Components of a Mission Statement

These benefits will occur only if the mission statement is effective. To be effective, the mission statement should have certain basic characteristics. It should be easy to read and understand, memorable, concise, and free of jargon. The organization should clearly articulate its responsibilities to each stakeholder so that each knows what to expect from the organization (Campbell and Yeung 1990). The mission statement should be inspirational (Bart 1998; Stone 1996). Inclusion of values makes a mission statement inspiring (Bangert 1997), but those values must be honestly held by the people in charge of the organization and the actions taken by all levels from the highest management on down must be in accordance with those values. Statements will be most inspiring if the values expressed agree with the values held by individual employees. If the purpose focuses on a higher ideal, all stakeholders will be proud to support it (Campbell and Yeung 1990; Caldeira 1997). The statement should include some element that identifies the organization and describes how it is unique from other, similar organizations, focusing on the organization's strengths and advantages. Although some feel that the mission statement should be brief, Campbell and Yeung (1990) suggest that length should not be a consideration because under that kind of constraint the mission statement will no longer reflect the culture of the organization, which comes through in the size, format, and wording of the statement—it is more important that it be a good read.

The mission statement should be written in such a way that it is meaningful. This means avoiding broad, general, or motherhood statements that could apply to any other organization. The mission statement should be measurable and actionable, so it can be seen whether the organization is achieving its mission and so employees can tell whether they are measuring up to behavioral expectations (Campbell and Yeung 1990). General, meaningless, and unmeasurable phrases to avoid include "world-class quality," "highest ethical standards," and "exceptional service to all" (the exceptional becomes routine) (Ehrenhalt 1997; Graham and Havlick 1994). Bailey (1996) notes that *measurable* does not have to mean "quantifiable"; qualitative measures can be used as well, as long as they are objective and reliable and as long as the time, labor, and other costs involved do not outweigh the benefits of the potential feedback. Specific qualitative measures include user satisfaction, quality of materials designed, or quality of programs. A measurable mission statement can last for generations, requiring constant striving even after the mission has been achieved. For example, a mission that includes getting people the information they need is measurable (how often were patrons satisfied?), but once achieved for one patron, it still needs to be achieved for all patrons who follow. Others suggest that the mission statement need not be measurable, but the objectives that come from it should be attainable (Stueart and Morgan 1987; Woods 1988).

All elements of the mission statement should be believable, achievable, and honest, explaining how promises will be fulfilled. If these qualities are missing, the statement lacks credibility and is not likely to influence or impress the very people it is aimed at. Unfortunately, when Bart (1997b) surveyed senior managers, he found that many times "the mission statement is itself a promise that appears to have been broken before the ink is dried" (12); not surprisingly, these managers were dissatisfied with the content and clarity of their mission statement. In order to have an impact on employee behavior, the employees must understand and believe in the statement (Caldeira 1997). Factors that make mission statements more credible include making the statement relevant to the organization's history and describing the physical and psychological limitations imposed on the organization by its environment (Dubberly 1983; Stone 1996). Environmental factors to consider include other organizations offering similar facilities, services, or programs; trends in technology; financial support; characteristics of suppliers and customers, defining the type of person who would consider coming to the organization; economic conditions, government regulations, and the impact these will have on future employees; and the mission and culture of the parent organization. The mission statement should complement the mission of the library's parent institution, describing how the library's goals allow the university or college to achieve its goals (Dust 1996). In a study of California academic library mission statements, Bangert (1997) found that values relating to the parent organization were frequently lacking, which she saw as a missed opportunity to articulate the library's uniqueness. "As Lynne Brindley has pointed out, 'the nature and character of an academic library cannot sensibly be considered in isolation from its institutional context, the mission and culture of the parent body'" (Brophy 1991, 146). Although most libraries will have similar purposes, their distinctiveness lies in how the libraries are run, which must be a reflection of the values of the parent institutions (Bangert 1997).

Libraries also need to make clear how they are different from other service points on campus such as the bookstore, the classroom, and the computer center (Hardesty, Hastreiter, and Henderson 1988). One way to do this is to identify the overlap between what the patron needs and what the library is able to provide (Stueart and Morgan 1987). To begin, though, Brophy (1991) suggests that librarians need to think of what business the library is in. As an example, he explains that a canal transportation business in the last century would have failed if it saw its mission as canal transport instead of transportation when railroads began to be built. Similarly, librarians should be in "the information or culture business rather than the library or book business" (136). Bangert (1997) suggests that library mission statements should include explanations of the services, resources, and competencies that are unique to the library, as well as cultural factors such as values and beliefs. Frequently mentioned elements found in Brophy's and Bangert's surveys of academic library mission statements include supporting the curriculum, supporting research and learning, collection development, teaching library skills, providing space for learning and study, providing access to local and global resources, diversity, leadership, organizing resources including the collection, preservation of heritage, using new technologies, staff development, behavioral suggestions such as friendliness, and values such as lifelong learning, critical thinking, and quality of teaching and service. Less common elements included resource management, scholarship, having a student focus, and accommodating adult learners. In its mission statement, the ACRL Undergraduate Librarians Discussion Group (1987) advocates innovation in the use of nontraditional technologies while supporting the needs of the students. The group notes that teaching students and supporting the curriculum are primary functions of the undergraduate library; however, Mosley (1988) warns that the mission statement must clarify what is meant by curriculum support in a way that describes how the library is unique on campus and what it is contributing to its parent institution. Similarly, Brophy (1991) advocates putting more detail and values into the generic idea of the provision of library services.

Writing the Mission Statement

The process of creating the mission statement should include representatives of all stakeholders, especially those who are critical to the mission's success: employees at all levels, customers, suppliers, and others with a vested interest, either as cowriters or to give criticism on proposed statements. Employees will be more motivated to reach their individual goals, which develop from the mission statement, if they are involved in the process of setting them (Woods 1988; Graham and Havlick 1994; Bart 1997a). Ironically, when Baetz and Bart (1996) and Bart (1997b) surveyed senior managers, they discovered that involving customers, nonmanagerial employees, and suppliers in the process was highly correlated with the managers' satisfaction with their mission statements, yet these people, who appear in these mission statements so that their interests are not ignored, are often excluded from the writing process. Similarly, students are most often left out of the process of developing academic library mission statements (Hardesty, Hastreiter, and Henderson 1985). Morrisey (1988) notes that a facilitator is very useful in diffusing dominant people, drawing out others, and ensuring that innovative thinking occurs. Most often, the library director is the primary drafter or chair of the committee (Hardesty, Hastreiter, and Henderson 1985,1988; Brophy 1991).

To avoid the angst involved with committee writing, statements can be written ahead of time by the facilitator or by committee members for the committee to critique (Harvey 1998; Bailey 1996). Albrecht (1994) advises committee members to think first of the basic ideas and to worry about the exact words much later, after the ideas are so condensed they can fit on the back of a business card. Questions to ask while creating the mission statement include (Bart 1998; Morrow 1996; Morrisey 1988; Porter 1997; Bailey 1996):

- What do we do, and why do we do it?
- What business are we in?
- Why does the organization exist?
- What is its true nature and purpose?
- What main services does the organization provide?
- Who is our primary customer?
- What is the organization's philosophy?
- What issues will be important in the future?
- What are our strengths and weaknesses?

- How are we different from others (technology, employees, management systems)?
- What makes us unique?
- What makes us successful?
- What are our responsibilities toward the board of directors, parent organization, legislative bodies, employees, customers, suppliers, general public, and others (specify)?
- What geographic areas do we serve?

Using a theme is an interesting way to format the mission statement and can be very effective in getting the reader involved while illustrating the culture of the organization. Instead of a dry listing of why an organization is wonderful, the theme mission statement tells a story that exemplifies the company's uniqueness, usually in a specific anecdote that focuses on why its employees are its strongest asset (Leuthesser and Kohli 1997).

After the mission statement is completed, the draft should be shown to all stakeholders for feedback and criticism (Bart 1998; Bailey 1996; Morrow 1996). In a survey of academic libraries, most mission statements (about 80%) were formally approved by a group or an individual (Hardesty, Hastreiter, and Henderson 1988). The mission statement should then be reviewed periodically to ensure that it remains an accurate reflection of the organization and that the goals that spring from it remain effective. Hardesty, Hastreiter, and Henderson (1985) found that libraries tended to review their mission statements every year, which corresponds to advice given to the business community (Morrisey 1988); goals and objectives should be reviewed more often (Dust 1996; Ireland and Hitt 1992; Cochran and David 1986). Campbell and Yeung (1990) caution against radical changes, comparing the mission statement to the United States Constitution: Change should be slow and should always be in line with the guiding principles first set out in the mission statement.

Using the Mission Statement Effectively

To be effective, the mission statement must be communicated to all stakeholders and, if necessary, clarified so that everyone understands it. If employees do not know where it is or what it says, the statement cannot be effective (Wright 1996). There are many ways the statement can be communicated: hung on posters or signs in conspicuous places where staff and patrons can see it every day, such as in lobbies, cafeterias, and meeting rooms; printed on bookmarks, stationary, paperweights, wallet-sized cards, or the backs of staff ID cards; added to brochures, booklets, annual reports, newsletters, and the university or college's catalog; included in packages given to new employees; and verbally affirmed in meetings or informal conversations between upper management and employees (Wright 1996; Graham and Havlick 1994; DeCandido 1995; Campbell and Yeung 1990; Morrisey 1988; Bart 1997a; Morrow 1996).

The statement must also be implemented. Goals, objectives, plans, and budgets should be written based on the mission statement. Woods (1988) advocates writing separate sets of goals and objectives for the organization, for each employee and, if needed, for each department. Elements within the mission statement should be reflected in recruitment, training, performance evaluations, rewards, promotions, and disciplinary actions (Stone 1996; Baetz and Bart 1996; Bart 1997a; Campbell and Yeung 1990). All major decisions should be made in reference to the mission statement to keep everyone working together (Ireland and Hitt 1992; Morrisey 1988; DeCandido 1995). Management must be living examples of the values and philosophy that appear in the mission statement and must be committed to supporting it (Stone 1996; Ireland and Hitt 1992; Graham and Havlick 1994).

The mission statement is effective if it helps employees do their jobs, if it is applied and accepted by all employees, and if employees are satisfied with it (Morrow 1996; Ireland and Hitt 1992; Bart 1997a). More concretely, Cochran, David, and Gibson (1985) and Cochran and David (1986) measured mission statement effectiveness by judging the degree to which they were inspiring and readable; readability was determined by calculations involving the number of words with three or more syllables and the number of words per sentence.

Examination of Three Library Mission Statements

In the past, many library missions were to "facilitate access to documents" (Penniman 1997, 11). Penniman advocates a change to a new mission, "to help current and future generations of citizens become independent problem solvers—who have available, and know how to use, information tools to address the challenges that face them, whether they are scholars, technicians, professionals, students, parents or lifelong learners of all ages. . . . The information industry has said its vision is to provide information anywhere, anytime. Librarians, I believe, must pursue yet a broader vision and assure a third component—for anyone" (12).

The academic library mission statements featured below were found on the Internet. They were chosen to represent a public university library (Walter E. Helmke Library, Indiana University, IPFW), a community college library (Lane Community College Library), and a private university library (Sadie A. Hartzler Library, Eastern Mennonite University).

The Mission Statements
Walter E. Helmke Library
Indiana University-Purdue University-Fort Wayne (IPFW)
http://www.lib.ipfw.edu/docs/library-info/collections/libmissn.html

Helmke Library Mission Statement
The Helmke Library's mission is to anticipate and support the needs of

IPFW's undergraduate and graduate students, faculty, administration, and professional community. The library is primarily committed to providing easy access to information and an atmosphere conducive to study and research; a collection development program that includes print, electronic, and other nonprint materials that directly support the needs of the undergraduate students, graduate students, and faculty of IPFW; access services for the timely retrieval of bibliographic data and materials from other information sources to support the research needs of the undergraduate students, graduate students and faculty; and expert professional information services that facilitate thorough and accurate use of the library's resources. In addition, the Helmke Library provides informational and other services for the university as a whole, including the operation of a University Archives. The Library also supports the university's mission by providing access to library materials and services to the community.

Approved as amended by Helmke Library Council, January 22, 1996.
Approved as amended by Senate Library Committee, May 1997

LCC Library
Lane Community College
http://lanecc.edu/library/princip.htm

Library Principles
The following four statements constitute the governing principles of Lane Community College Library. They were adopted by the Library staff from 1992 to the present.
- Mission and Philosophy
- Unifying Principles
- Purpose and Goals
- Library Bill of Rights [from the American Library Association; not reproduced here]

Library Mission and Philosophy
Lane Community College is a comprehensive community college whose mission is to provide accessible, high quality, and affordable lifelong education. Within this context, the primary goal of the Library is to provide library services that support the curriculum and fulfill the information needs of students, faculty, staff, administration, and community through the building and maintaining of a vital collection of library materials and resources. Whenever possible, these will be extended to the community.

Library Unifying Principles
In our interactions with patrons:
- We believe our patrons should be treated with professionalism and respect.

- . We believe the Library should be accessible to everyone.
- We believe the Library should provide an environment conducive to learning and productive work.
- We believe in promoting library literacy.
- We believe in the use of plain, simple language.

In our interactions with our colleagues:

- We will endeavor to apply the above principles.
- We will endeavor to understand each other's work and recognize each other's areas of expertise.
- We will endeavor to foster a team approach to meeting the challenges of our work.
- We will endeavor to operate under the principles of consensual decision making.

Library Purpose and Goals

In support of the stated goals and objectives of the College, the Library is developing a unified program of library-media resources and services. The purpose of this program is to enhance instruction and learning in a manner consistent with the philosophy and curriculum of Lane Community College. The Library is guided by the principles of the Library Bill of Rights in the development of its programs and services.

The goals of the Library are:

- To provide organized collections of print and non-print resources which will meet institutional and instructional requirements as well as the individual needs of students.
- To create an environment in which resources are made readily accessible, not only through the provision of appropriate facilities, furnishings, equipment, and supplies, but particularly through the provision of adequate staff.
- To facilitate learning and community services by providing services, resources and facilities which encourage and stimulate individualized instruction, independent study and effective use of resources by students, faculty and the community.

Sadie A. Hartzler Library

Eastern Mennonite University
http://www.emu.edu/library/mission.html

Sadie A. Hartzler Library: Mission

Eastern Mennonite University offers accredited academic programs in the arts and sciences, graduate theological education, and selected graduate degrees. Eastern Mennonite University seeks to glorify God, to pursue excellence in all educational programs, and to challenge students to answer Christ's call to a life of witness, service, and peacemaking.

The Sadie A. Hartzler Library supports the mission of Eastern Mennonite University by providing information resources needed for baccalaureate and graduate education in an Anabaptist/Mennonite Christian context, and by advocating and enabling information literacy—the ability to find, evaluate, and use information effectively.

The library serves these information needs by:
- providing a well-trained, service-oriented staff who can interpret and teach access to, evaluation of, and use of information resources;
- collecting, preserving, and making accessible a core collection of materials in all relevant formats; and
- providing access to information resources:
  - ~ through online catalogs, indexes, and databases;
  - ~ through connections to local, regional, and global networks; and
  - ~ by securing materials for students, faculty, and staff through interlibrary loan and other resource sharing arrangements.

Since learning requires critical analysis, diverse expression, and exposure to a multiplicity of perspectives, a variety of viewpoints will be represented in the library collection.

Discussion of Featured Mission Statements

In telephone conversations with librarians who were involved in the creation of these mission statements (Judith Violette, library director at Walter E. Helmke Library at Indiana-Purdue-Fort Wayne (IPFW); Don Macnaughtan, reference librarian at Lane Community College Library; and Boyd Reese, director of libraries for Sadie A. Hartzler Library at Eastern Mennonite University), the comment that came up again and again was that the process itself was extremely useful. Thinking about the issues helped to clarify what the library was trying to achieve, and the discussions were a means for new directors to get to know their staff and establish expectations. Judith Violette explained that when the librarians at Helmke Library revised their mission statement and collection development policy, they took the documents to the faculty library committee for approval, partly to force a discussion with faculty about the library's limited budget and its undergraduate focus: "I saw the development of the mission statement as every bit as important as the statement itself because the development of it allowed us to discuss with the faculty things like well, yes, you'd like us to be a research library, but these are the budget constraints. How do you want that to be reflected in the statement? Yes, you'd like us to have a world-class periodical collection, but what does that really mean in terms of the constraints that we have? We were able bring in budget issues, we were able to bring in format issues, we were able to bring in issues of how we relate to the community in our discussions with faculty; and I thought that was very important." The faculty asked for some changes to the mission statement: "Our support of faculty research was through the part of the mission state-

ment that says document delivery or access service, we're talking about retrieval of materials, and the faculty didn't want it there, they wanted to be
included in all of the other statements, that we directly support the needs of
undergraduate students, graduate students, and faculty of IPFW." This
change had a small impact on how the collection is developed: Their book
budget now pays for providing access to new research databases and the
document delivery components for some of them, but they have not attempted to purchase books to support faculty research.

There was some variation in the composition of each mission statement committee, but all found the writing process to be nonconfrontational,
though finding the perfect words that everyone could agree on was often a
challenge. The group at Lane Community College Library, which operates
with a nonhierarchical, shared decision-making structure, was composed
of five librarians and nine support staff, and the statement gestated for about
three years, then took a couple of months to write. At Helmke Library,
IPFW, all of the librarians were involved in the writing, with support staff
only peripherally involved, and the revision process took about six months.
The entire library staff was involved at Hartzler Library, Eastern Mennonite University, where the director wrote an initial draft and the staff changed
it and added to it, with rest periods for reflection; it was completed within a
four month semester. Interestingly, Hardesty, Hastreiter, and Henderson
(1985) found that most statements took a week to four months to develop
from initial draft to adoption.

Students were not involved in writing or critiquing any of the mission
statements, although all three librarians saw students as being the central
benefactor of their statement and the main priority of their library. "We do
view ourselves as an undergraduate institution," Violette explained. "We do
feel strongly that we have to make the library attractive to students so that
it's not just a warehouse or a big research collection. But it also has to be a
place where students might be invited to go, to go and browse around and
learn more, as well as a place where we provide the emphasis on providing
information and service to undergraduates." Boyd Reese agrees: "At the most
fundamental level, the students' needs are the reason for being for the library. . . . [The] primary purpose of our library is to support the curriculum. We can assist other people like faculty, but they'll need to go outside
for what we [don't have]. So everything we do, all of our services, our whole
collection, is aimed at the student population that we serve." The mission
statements have not generated much interest among the students, most of
whom are probably unaware that the mission statement exists. As we saw
above, this kind of missed opportunity was common in the literature.

In writing the mission statement, both Violette and Macnaughtan de-
clared that part of the challenge was to keep it broad or flexible enough to
allow for a wide range of specific actions, such as switching between access
and ownership, and to allow for changing technology, such as moving from

CD-ROMs to Web-based databases. Although this generality is not very helpful when dealing with specific collection development decisions, it does provide the framework for specific policies and other resource allocation decisions such as whether to put in disabled access stations. Reading from his mission statement, Macnaughtan commented, "'We believe in the use of plain, simple language,' well, that's kind of like saying you believe in apple pie, but what we were trying to get away from was jargon and bureaucracy and all those other things that bedevil some libraries." As a mission statement element, this phrase meets all of the criteria discussed above for effectiveness: it's memorable, clear, measurable, and it reflects the culture, values, and beliefs of the library's employees. One benefit of a broad mission statement is that it will not need to be altered very often. Macnaughtan compared LCC Library's principles to the United States Constitution, "and how often do we mess with the Constitution, not too often." Violette also anticipated that her library's mission statement will not need much revising.

All three statements reflected their libraries' uniqueness and referred to their parent institutions' mission statements. Hartzler Library's mission statement is an excellent example of this; as Reese expresses it, "We integrally tied our mission into the broader institutional mission." He explained that they were trying "to provide a rationale for the services that we do, the staff that we need, the collection that we need to support the needs of an institution our size." Although they did not feel the need to have their mission statement formally approved, Reese forwarded a draft to the dean for his comments. The staff at LCC Library based their mission statement on the college's mission statement, then, Macnaughtan expounded, "put down a set of beliefs, really, interactions with patrons as a set of beliefs, and our interactions with each other as a set of expectations. . . how to provide excellent service and how we could treat each other the best way. Those were the two factors we were looking at, and being efficient and being conscientious and being thoughtful and kind to patrons and each other." In keeping with this internal as well as external focus, new employees at LCC Library are given the principles to read during orientation as part of the process of fitting into the library's culture. "It's not something we would refer to every day, this is probably the first time I've looked at it in some months, but it's always at the back of everyone's mind, and what it's really doing is giving people expectations of what they should and what they shouldn't work up to, and what they can expect from each other and expect with ways we should treat the patrons," Macnaughtan said, and it seems to be working: performance at the library has improved since the first policies were written. LCC Library's mission statement on the Web includes a link to the college's mission statement and reproduces the ALA Library Bill of Rights. Violette confessed that the librarians at Helmke Library based their statement on Earlham College Library's statement, changing it to reflect the

IPFW environment; and Helmke Library, which, unlike the private liberal arts college library, is a public university library that serves the community, supports faculty research and undergraduate as well as graduate study, has a university archives, and is an independent unit within a larger library system. Including unique, distinguishing elements in the mission statement, such as how the library fits into the culture of the parent organization, is essential if the statement is to be effective.

All three mission statements were published on the Internet. In addition to this, new employees at LCC Library receive copies of the principles and Helmke Library's mission statement is included in brochures about the library and guides to services. Violette noted, "I use the mission statement a lot when I ask for additional staffing and things of that sort or when we talk about programs or priorities or things of that sort, and [administrators] like to hear that, they like to think that what we're doing is in accordance with what we've said we're going to do. . . . We have tried very hard to fashion our objectives and goals around this mission statement." Boyd Reese finds his mission statement useful in guiding decisions "in terms of allocating things like the need for different staff, the importance of activities like preservation, the importance of access to various things, and the need to increase funding for things like online resources," as well as asking for more staff and adjusting staff duties. Reese also points to his mission statement when talking to faculty committees and administrators; he feels that the mission statement indicates that "we have a clear idea of what we're trying to do here, and [we] want to do it, so therefore my request for resources is not unreasonable."

All three librarians felt that the effort of creating a mission statement was worthwhile. Performance has improved at LCC Library, where employees are living up to the expectations that they helped to set and new employees are clear about what is expected from them. Each statement sets a solid foundation for requesting resources from administrators and faculty committees: Reese and Violette used their mission statements effectively, gaining new staff members, reallocating staff time, and providing access to new databases and other resources. Reese adds, "I think it has helped us understand more clearly what our goals are. That's in a broad sense, it's like a broad collection development policy that's not going to help you decide to add one item versus another item, or add neither, or add both; but in terms of what we do overall, I think it's been very helpful."

Conclusion

We have seen that mission statements can be valuable documents. However, they are not magical elixirs: their strength lies in how they are created, how they are implemented, how they are communicated, and, to a smaller degree, what elements are included. To be an effective guide, the mission statement must be an accurate reflection of the unique culture of the library and of the parent institution, addressing their purposes, values, and beliefs. Writing and then implementing a mission statement involves a substantial investment of time and effort, but if done correctly, this investment will yield great returns.

References

ACRL Undergraduate Librarians Discussion Group and the ULS Steering Committee. 1987. The mission of a university undergraduate library: Model statement. *College & Research Libraries News* 48(9):542–44.

Albrecht, Karl. 1994. *The Northbound Train: Finding the Purpose, Setting the Direction, Shaping the Destiny of Your Organization.* New York: Amacom.

Baetz, Mark C., and Christopher K. Bart. 1996. Developing mission statements which work. *Long Range Planning* 29(4):526–33.

Bailey, James A. 1996. Measuring your mission. *Management Accounting* 78(6):44–46.

Bangert, Stephanie Rogers. 1997. Values in college and university library mission statements: A search for distinctive beliefs, meaning, and organizational culture. Vol. 21 of *Advances in Librarianship*, ed. Irene Godden. San Diego, Calif.: Academic Press, 91–106.

Bart, Christopher K. 1996. The impact of mission on firm innovativeness. *International Journal of Technology Management*, Special Issue on the 5th International Forum on Technology Management 11(3/4):479–93.

———. 1997a. Mission possible. *CA Magazine* 130(7):33–34.

———. 1997b. Sex, lies and mission statements. *Business Horizons* 40(6):9–18.

———. 1998. Mission matters. *CA Magazine* 103(2):31–32, 41.

Brophy, Peter. 1991. The mission of the academic library. *British Journal of Academic Librarianship* 6(3):135–47.

Caldeira, Edward. 1997. How a written mission statement helps employees and the company. *Professional Builder* 62(10):32.

Calfee, David L. 1993. Get your mission statement working! *Management Review* 82(1):54–57.

Campbell, Andrew. 1997. Mission statements. *Long Range Planning* 30(6):931–32.

Campbell, Andrew, and Sally Yeung. 1990. *Do You Need a Mission Statement?* London: Economist Publications.

Cochran, Daniel S., and Fred R. David. 1986. Communication effectiveness of organizational mission statements. *Journal of Applied Communication Research* 14(2):108–18.

Cochran, Daniel S., Fred R. David, and C. Kendrick Gibson. 1985. A framework for developing an effective mission statement. *Journal of Business Strategies* 2(2):4–17.

DeCandido, GraceAnne Andreassi. 1995. Your mission, should you choose to accept it. *Wilson Library Bulletin* 69(7):6.

Dubberly, Ronald A. 1983. Why you must know your library's mission. *Public Libraries* 22(3):89–90.

Dust, Bob. 1996. Making mission statements meaningful. *Training & Development* 50(6):53.

Ehrenhalt, Alan. 1997. In search of a world-class mission statement. *Governing* 10(6):7–8.

Goett, Pamela. 1997. Mission impossible. *Journal of Business Strategy* 18(1):2.

Graham, John W., and Wendy C. Havlick. 1994. *Mission Statements: A Guide to the Corporate and Nonprofit Sectors.* New York: Garland Publishing.

Hardesty, Larry L., Jamie Hastreiter, and David Henderson. 1985. *Mission Statements for College Libraries: Clip Note #5.* Chicago: Association of College and Research Libraries.

———. 1988. Development of college library mission statements. *Journal of Library Administration* 9(3):11–34.

Harvey, Stuart J. 1998. A practical approach to stating your 'mission.' *Management Review* 87(1):F1, F3.

Ireland, R. Duane, and Michael A. Hitt. 1992. Mission statements: Importance, challenge, and recommendations for development. *Business Horizons* 35(3):34–42.

Leisner, Tony. 1986. Mission statements and the marketing mix. *Public Libraries* 25 (fall):86–87.

Leuthesser, Lance, and Chiranjeev Kohli. 1997. Corporate identity: The role of mission statements. *Business Horizons* 40(3):59–66.

Morrisey, George L. 1988. Who needs a mission statement? You do: How to go about devising your reason for being. *Training and Development Journal* 42(3):50–52.

Morrow, Edwin P. 1996. The planner's mission. *Journal of Financial Planning* 9(2):83–84.

Mosley, Madison M. 1988. Mission statements for the community college LRC. *College and Research Libraries News* 49(10):653–54.

Penniman, W. David. 1997. Strategic positioning of information services in a competitive environment. *Bulletin of the American Society for Information Science* 23(4):11–14.

Porter, Monroe. 1997. Mission statement is a valuable marketing tool. *Contractor* 44(11):38.

Stone, Romuald A. 1996. Mission statements revisited. *SAM Advanced Management Journal* 61(1):31–37.

Stueart, Robert D., and Barbara B. Morgan. 1987. *Library Management.* 3d ed. Littleton, Colo.: Libraries Unlimited.

Vardi, Yaov, Yoash Wiener, and Micha Popper. 1989. The value content of organizational mission as a factor in the commitment of members. *Psychological Reports* 65(1):27–34.

Woods, L. B. 1988. Mission statements, organizational goals, and objectives. *Arkansas Libraries* 45 (June):13–17.

Wright, J. Nevan. 1996. Creating a quality culture. *Journal of General Management* 21(3):19–29.

Holistic Approach to Diversity:
Practical Projects for Promoting Inclusivity

Arglenda Friday

Introduction

Libraries can use many approaches to promote inclusion of diverse groups. Several practical projects and activities have been created and implemented with varying degrees of success at San Jose State University (SJSU).

Following a brief definition of the "holistic" approach, the diversity initiative objectives, strategies, and avenues for action and implementation are explored as they relate to creating opportunities for library collaboration and participation. Background demographics help illustrate the context within which the activities took place. The report concludes with a description of sample projects.

It should be noted that the university is located in a region of the country that is rich with diversity. This location has been a major advantage for promoting the diversity initiative; however, the projects can be replicated or implemented in other areas with less diverse demographics. Minor adjustments that may need to be made in the projects will be noted in the text.

Holistic Approach

According to the *Random House Webster's College Dictionary* (1997), the holistic approach is based on the theory that whole entities have an existence other than as the mere sum of their parts. The third edition of the *Heritage Dictionary of the English Language* (1992) further defines *holism* as a complete system composed of elements emphasizing the importance of the whole and the interdependence of interacting wholes that are more than the mere sum of the elementary particles. Thus defined and applied to the library diversity initiative, a holistic approach is advocated primarily because of the strong interdependence of the different groups within the urban university community and the campus environment. In addition to being more powerful and inclusive than a single unit, holism can also be economically advantageous for all participants because of shared costs and expenses.

Diversity is defined broadly to address differences as well as similarities among entities. The criteria used for consideration of groups in our initiative included, but was not limited to:
- ability and disability (persons with various abilities);
- age (traditional students, reentry or older students, young adults, adults, seniors, and children);
- citizenship (native born or international students);
- class (lower, middle, upper, and intermediate subgroups);

- country of origin as well as country of upbringing;
- culture (cultural upbringing or preference);
- educational level (reentry, traditional, graduate, undergraduate);
- ethnicity (major groups and subgroups within);
- gender/status (heterosexual, gay or lesbian, bisexual, transgendered, other);
- generations (first, second, older, younger, X,Y,Z);
- language (primary, secondary, other);
- learning style (audio, visual);
- race (census identification or self identification);
- religion or religious preference;
- seasons (equinoxes, harvests, and cultural festivals linked to seasonal changes);
- status (student, staff, faculty, administrator, or local).

The criteria for diversity were expanded to include the seasons because there are often cultural festivals or rituals associated with the solstices, such as the green corn festival or autumn harvest or spring for renewal and rebirth.

Another aspect of the holistic approach—economy of scale—is to include as many sponsors or collaborators as possible. Broad sponsorship can increase the pool of resources and widen the market share for advertisements, thereby improving the visibility of the service or event while enhancing the exposure or image of the library. Likewise, the workload can be spread over a large group to lessen the demands on individuals. Although this disbursal of responsibilities can work to the advantage of the coordinator, scheduling meetings for a large group can be challenging. However, using a small core group, delegating responsibilities, creating a broad and effective communication network, and diligently monitoring assignments are critical to successful endeavors.

Objectives

The demographics and variety of cultures in California and San Jose are quite conducive to taking a holistic approach to a diversity initiative. The holistic approach to diversity can accomplish several objectives for the library as well as the university community and outside sponsors. For the most part, this approach provides opportunities for creativity and community involvement that can promote positive images of the library. Likewise, library personnel can assume proactive roles for the institution while networking with other groups and agencies to jointly sponsor functions. The outreach effort can also be used to publicize the library's collections and services.

The primary objective of the diversity initiative is to find or create activities and events that provide occasions for promoting inclusivity of diverse groups at several different levels and arenas. The chief operative is to increase knowledge and awareness of our similarities and differences in order that we might be more respectful of our differences while capitalizing on our similarities and common interests.

To be effective in promoting the diversity initiative, library personnel should be not only committed to diversity, but also knowledgeable of other cultures and groups under consideration or at least willing to learn about them. Staff should also be willing to get involved in all stages of the process from the user needs assessment through planning, implementation, and debriefing sessions following the program or event.

Another objective of the holistic approach is inclusivity, meaning "target" groups for consideration should be selected according to broad-based guidelines. The SJSU diversity umbrella is very wide because there are so many different groups in its environment. For example, its Asian and Asian Pacific population consists of large numbers of Vietnamese, Philipino, Hmong, Chinese, Japanese, Korean, Taiwanese, and other subgroups, in addition to many students of mixed heritage. With such demographics, it is easy to sponsor or fund several Asian activities as there is an adequate number of students, personnel, and community groups to support them. Libraries with smaller populations may wish to focus on major cultural observations or events that generate large patronage and backing.

Proactivism is encouraged along with emphasis on networking and generating the support of key players such as administrators, students and student groups, staff, faculty, business and community organizations, and other interested parties. Their cooperation and support is critical for an effective program. Key players include library and university administrators as well as decision makers in the community because they are possible funding sources, event promoters, and joint sponsors. Input from the target groups is also an important requisite for successful diversity projects.

Visibility and positive image are equally important goals of the holistic approach. Active involvement in diversity programs should be used to show everyone that library personnel are not only knowledgeable of diversity but also committed to the cause of promoting inclusivity, understanding, and mutual respect among all cultures.

Background Demographics
State of California

According to the U.S. Bureau of the Census population data, California is the most populous state in the union with more than 32 million residents. The racial and ethnic distribution ranks Euro Americans at 18 million (54%), followed by Hispanics at 8 million (26%). Persons of Hispanic origin consist primarily of Mexicans but include Puerto Ricans, Cubans, and others. Likewise, the group of Asian and Pacific Islanders at 9.6 percent consists of several subgroups. Smaller populations of African Americans at 7.4 percent, American Indians at 1 percent, and a large group of "others and unknown comprising 2 percent complete the tally. It should be noted that the proportion of the population speaking a language other than English at home is almost one third (31.5%).

Regional, County, and City Demographics

The region, often referred to as the Bay Area, is also noted for its ethnic diversity. With more than 1.6 million people, Santa Clara County population has less diversity than the state with about 62 percent Anglo, 19 percent Hispanic, and 4 percent African American. However, the city of San Jose has demographics more representative of the state. Of the twenty-nine California cities of over 50,000 with no ethnic majority, nine are in the Bay Area, and two, San Jose and Milpitas, are in Santa Clara County (Horner, 1998).

As California's second largest city, San Jose, like four of California's five largest cities, no longer has an ethnic majority. According to 1997 data, San Jose has almost one million people. Of this number 53 percent of the population (491,000) is Anglo, followed by Hispanics at 24 percent, Asians and Pacific Islanders with 18 percent, and African Americans at 4 percent. The number of American Indians in the Santa Clara Valley totals more than 30,000 persons representing about a hundred tribes.

Enrollment Demographics

Student enrollment in California colleges and universities reflects the diversity of the state. Records in the *Chronicle of Higher Education* list more than 500,000 students matriculating at public four-year institutions, although twice that number attend public community colleges. Of these numbers, 55 percent of the students are women and 49 percent are ethnic minorities. In public four-year and two-year institutions, the percentages of minority students are 51.1 percent and 50.5 percent, respectively.

San Jose State University (SJSU) is one of the larger institutions in the twenty-four-campus California State University system. Surpassed only by CSU Long Beach and San Diego State, SJSU has an enrollment of more than 26,000 students. The campus is located in downtown San Jose, in the heart of Silicon Valley and Santa Clara County. Founded in 1857, SJSU is the oldest university in the CSU system. It has a long, rich history that has been enhanced by its location in a region recognized for cutting-edge technology and innovations in the global economy.

Demographics by ethnicity for SJSU are similar to those for the state. However, SJSU enrollment figures for other diverse groups may vary somewhat. For example, the number of students and personnel with physical disabilities is relatively high—probably because of the small, compact campus and the close proximity to public transportation. Likewise, the urban location attracts more nontraditional students, such as older students with families, and individuals who work in the downtown area. According to the university profile, the modal SJSU undergraduate is almost twenty-five years old and a resident of Santa Clara County. Many of the students attended local high schools and transferred from the one of the ten local community colleges. Given the high cost of living in the area, most students are employed full-time.

The diverse enrollment at SJSU is composed of 54 percent female, 5 percent African American, 29 percent Asian, 6 percent Philipino, 10 percent Mexican American, 4 percent other Latino, 1 percent American Indian/Alaskan, 33 percent Anglo, and 12 percent not stated. About 20 percent are graduate students and 64 percent are full-time.

The faculty of 1,650 is less diverse but includes people of color and persons of various sexual orientations or status and abilities. Staff and support personnel are much more reflective of the student enrollment and local demographics.

Primary language is another variable for consideration. About one-third of all undergraduates did not speak English as the primary language at age six, and another 13 percent had at least one parent for whom English was not the native language. Although most of the students are U.S. citizens and California residents, SJSU has a relatively large international student and "immigrant" enrollment. The majority of the international students are from the Republic of China, and most immigrant students report Vietnam as their country of origin.

Clark Library and the Instructional Resource Center
For several years, the library and instructional resource center (IRC) functioned as a single unit. Combined personnel for both facilities total almost two hundred students from all ethnic groups, twenty-eight faculty, and eighty support staff. Thus, ethnic diversity in the library/IRC is achieved primarily with student assistants and support personnel, as there is minimal diversity in the faculty and administrative ranks.

Strategies and Avenues for Action
Strategies
Several strategies can be used to promote the holistic approach. The best design—and most obvious avenue for action—is to pursue the many opportunities generated by the sheer diversity of the region. Ethnic celebrations, religious events, and cultural activities can provide excellent possibilities for collaboration with community groups, student organizations, and outside sponsors.

A supportive administration has been the other catalyst for exploring diversity objectives. Both the California State University System through the chancellor and the campus community through the Campus Climate Committee created by the university president have been the key players in the initiative. In addition to allocating funds for diversity work, they have also encouraged staff involvement through release time and incentive grants. The library continues to be a leader in the diversity effort, primarily because of the clientele and personnel.

Student employees are an important element and can be strong supporters of the diversity effort. Rosen et al (1994) in the article, "Student Employees and the Academic Library's Multicultural Mission," reference several similarly successful strategies used at Bowling Green State University to recruit minority student employees. Fortunately, SJSU has a diverse student assistant pool, thus it simply needed to survey them to determine their interests and desired degree of participation in its programs.

Given the support of key players, strategies for promoting diversity need to be examined. The strategies used most often and with the highest degree of success consisted of the following:

1. Examining the environment for key components. What are the issues or needs to be addressed? Who are the parties we need to involve? What are our clearly defined objectives and goals? Who is our target or intended market or audience?

2. Gathering information to determine what activities to pursue. Surveys were used to determine the demographic composition of our target market, and need assessments were used to determine what issues warranted consideration, followed by a prioritization of the issues.

3. Generating ideas for projects and activities, followed by a feasibility analysis to determine which were affordable and achievable. It is also good to establish a time frame for action at this stage.

4. After the project or activity, a debriefing or evaluation is needed to determine what worked well along with a more serious discussion of those items that were not successful. Feedback from a variety of sources is recommended with particular note given to constructive criticism and comments from the targeted group, along with suggestions for ways to improve the next venture.

5. Regular review of ongoing projects is recommended to help avoid burnout by the service providers and loss of interest by the participants. To balance the analysis, reviews should be made by both insiders and persons outside the organization.

6. Evaluation of all projects is necessary to determine the impact of the activities on the participants and the service providers. It can also be used to provide data and comments for revisions and improvement as well as for documentation that may be required for grant proposals and funding sources.

7. Finally, based on the evaluation and feedback, activities can be modified or adjusted, revised or enhanced, or, in some cases, eliminated.

Needs assessment and surveys of target groups are critical components of the planning stage. Input from these groups can be gleaned using surveys and focus groups and by working closely with key members of these organizations. In addition, the opportunistic route of joint collaboration with these target groups can be used to acknowledge and maximize publicity and attendance for different celebrations—ethnic, religious, seasonal, international, global, regional, local, and special events.

Another aspect of the opportunistic method is the possibility for securing grants and additional funds for programming through collaboration, networking, and joint sponsorship with the targeted groups, particularly nonprofit organizations.

Avenues for Action

Many of the projects were easy to generate because the avenues for action were nicely paved superhighways. Ethnic celebrations, religious events, and international activities are good places to start, particularly if there is national and international recognition of the events. Possibilities include Kwaanza, TET or Vietnamese New Year, Juneteenth, Chinese New Year, Women's History Month, Treaty of Guadalupe Hidalgo, Cinco de Mayo, Native American Heritage Month, African American Heritage Month, Ramadan, Rosh Hashana or the Jewish New Year, and others. Regional and local festivals are equally appealing if there is strong community identification with the event.

Another avenue that is growing in popularity is library sponsorship or joint hosting of authors' teas or readings by ethnic authors. Likewise, if an adequate number of ethnic book vendors is in the region, book fairs can be jointly sponsored with the library to promote sales of ethnic materials and perhaps increase donations of materials to the host library.

Regardless of the avenue taken or the strategy used to promote diversity, evaluation and assessment of the outcomes is important to a successful campaign. Review by insiders as well as outsiders is critical because the responses provide feedback and suggestions. In like manner, successful events can become annual events and possible fundraisers, with proper planning, networking, and support from the participants.

Sample Projects and Activities

Many of the programs in the SJSU diversity initiative can be replicated in other libraries. For regions with less diversity, major recognized ethnic holidays may be acknowledged with support from community organizations. In some areas, churches and schools are more reliable joint sponsors because they generally have loyal followings. Seasonal events are equally good starter projects because many ethnic groups associate seasonal changes with important events such as autumn harvests or spring rebirths and renewals. Finally, as was previously mentioned, when in doubt, recruit key members from the targeted group to get input and ascertain the cultural appropriateness of the proposal.

Applying the holistic approach, primary emphasis is placed on seeking and creating opportunities to acknowledge and celebrate diversity while promoting inclusion and validation of all groups. Further, using the above-referenced strategies and avenues for action, the following projects, activities, and events were created as part of SJSU's diversity initiative at the different levels.

State Level

Ethnic Resource Centers: During the late 1980s and early 1990s, there were several meetings held and considerable discussion with the California Library Services Board and members of the library community about creating Ethnic Resource Centers to complement the California State Library Association (CSLA) System Reference Services Program. The Ethnic Resource Centers were to be one component of the service program.

Several models were proposed for the centers, along with numerous locations throughout the state. Based on the changing demographics of the state, the objective of the centers was to enhance and expand information services to ethnic populations while developing and increasing collections by and about diverse groups.

Although the primary focus was on public libraries, several representatives from university libraries were active members and participants in the forums and discussions as there were many opportunities for collaboration and cooperative effort. Unfortunately, the grand plan was not implemented, although an ethnic resource center of sorts was created at one of the sites. Nevertheless, participants were able to network and explore ideas generated from the discussion groups. It would also appear that if the demographics of the state continue the current trend, there may be occasion to revisit this proposal.

Scholarship and Mentoring Program: The Library Development Services Bureau of the California State Library sponsors the Multi-Ethnic Recruitment Scholarship Program to increase the number of ethnic students in the pipeline. Candidates are nominated by the library, the library system, or the library school.

Candidates with experience working with ethnic groups and communities are sought for the program. Experience is broadly defined to include work with ESL students, Head Start children, migrant workers, and service organizations working with ethnic communities. Research projects and internships are included in this program.

This project can easily be replicated in other states, particularly if there are strong ethnic caucuses or library chapters and friends groups at the state level. For example, both the northern and southern chapters of the California Librarians Black Caucus offer scholarships to African American students for library school. Worthy of note is the action plan and model statement for public libraries to create a model for statewide service promoted by the Colorado Librarians (Alire 1997a). Their comprehensive plan focused on "visible" ethnic populations as the related target markets.

Caucuses and ethnic groups in other states can consider petitioning the state library association for diversity scholarship funding or may jointly fund scholarships for ethnic students and employees that might be interested in pursuing additional library training or even library and information science degrees. Similar programs and collaborative sponsorships provide mentors for potential and current library school students.

Mentoring should be an important component of any scholarship program or diversity initiative for two big reasons. First, mentoring can usually be done with minimal cost or initial outlay of funds. The time commitment, however, can be lengthy for both mentor and mentee. Second, many ethnic students are the first members of their families to attend college or pursue graduate degrees, so there is usually a strong need for a support system, particularly if a familial support system is lacking (Alire 1997b).

Professional Organizations: Another opportunity for comparing notes on diversity programs occurs among diversity-oriented groups of professional library organizations. Several ethnic-specific organizations are within the state for Latino librarians (REFORMA), African Americans (Black Caucus), and Asian Americans (CALA), as well as interest groups affiliated with state and national library associations.

Annual state library conferences, such as the California Library Association (CLA) Annual Conference and regional or special interest group programs, offer excellent forums for comparing notes and discussing activities. Conferences also provide opportunities for networking and helping library school students develop professionally by inviting them to participate in the programs.

Regional Level

The sheer diversity of the Bay Area has provided numerous opportunities to collaborate with other groups. The library was able to host an exhibit of the Asian essays and art as part of the traveling collection of the Growing Up Asian in America program. The program, sponsored by the Asian Pacific American Community Fund in San Francisco, has now become an annual event with prizes and awards donated by major corporate sponsors.

Joint campus sponsors included the California Faculty Association, the College of Education, Asian American Studies, Campus Climate Diversity Committee, and the Faculty Enhancement Council. In some years, SJSU participation has been amplified by featuring contest winners who are also students at SJSU.

Because other libraries were included in the list of sponsors of the traveling exhibit, SJSU was able to exchange information and resource guides with the public libraries to enhance both displays. Likewise, participants were able to share transportation costs between locations and municipalities.

The relatively large Asian population in the Bay Area and the corporate sponsorship of the prizes greatly contributed to the success of this endeavor. However, other states and locales can sponsor essay contests centered on the same theme, which chiefly addressed what it means to be ethnically diverse in America by working with local schools and corporations. The programs can be modified by age group to include essays for older students and arts/crafts projects for younger participants.

California State University System Level
The chancellor's office sponsors a number of diversity projects for the twenty-four campuses within the CSU system. As most of the programs are for the entire campus, the library can take a strong lead in grant-writing and participation because it serves the entire campus community, as opposed to individual colleges that may serve smaller segments of the student populace.

Librarians have written and secured grants for collection development, diversity workshops, cultural sensitivity training, and programs on cultural pluralism. Given the broad guidelines for the system grants, librarians have been able to secure funding for CD-ROMs and electronic resources such as Ethnic NewsWatch or ethnic and gender-specific databases for Chicanos, African or Asian Americans, and Women's studies programs.

Community Level and Local Arenas
The ethnic composition of Santa Clara Valley and the city of San Jose provides numerous opportunities for collaboration and joint sponsorship of cultural events, exhibits, and workshops.

City Workshops: The library participated in an Anti-Graffiti Program sponsored by the city of San Jose. A librarian did a workshop on how to locate resources and funding opportunities for neighborhood and community activism. The session entitled SHOW ME THE MONEY included Web sites as well as samples of successful grant proposals for the diverse audience.

As a public institution, many workshop attendees were unaware of their "rights" as taxpayers to use the university library, so this public relations effort provided information and goodwill to the community. Other libraries, particularly main public libraries, can get involved in similar events and informative functions sponsored by the city given their usual close proximity to city hall or the civic center. Mailing costs and publicity may also be defrayed if the library can use interdepartmental or city mailing facilities to advertise programs.

Ethnic Book Fairs and Authors: Many lesser-known ethnic authors are not supported by the large presses. This oversight has given rise to a number of minority book dealers and small presses. If librarians are aware of local small and ethnic presses and have good working relationships with them, they can be in an ideal position to sponsor ethnic book fairs and autograph parties for local ethnic authors.

SJSU successfully hosted a minority book and resource fair with the support and participation of local vendors. Considerable planning and advertising may be needed to guarantee large audiences, but book fairs can provide good-will and be financially rewarding for the vendors and the libraries. Dependent on the selling contracts or agreements, libraries can bargain for a share of the profits or book donations for the diversity collection.

Autograph parties and book talks for minority authors can be successful endeavors as well. The event can be linked with an ethnic heritage month or ethnic-specific event to spread the advertising costs and increase attendance. For example, female authors can be featured in March as part of the community or library acknowledgment of Women's History Month. To minimize costs and develop a following, a library may want to start with local authors and book clubs. Another option is to court a hometown author who has a top seller and use the event as a fundraiser for scholarships and collection enhancement. With foresight, good public relations, and ingenuity, the possibilities are limitless.

University or Campus Level

The SJSU administration and community supports many projects and programs to develop, implement, evaluate, and monitor an institution-wide plan aimed at achieving a nurturing and effective climate in which diverse populations will flourish. The library has been an active participant in several of these programs in a number of capacities.

Campus Climate: As a university committee charged with advising the administration on the status of diversity mandates, the hundred-person committee has broad representation from many of the diverse groups on campus, including faculty, staff, administrators, and students. The library had a representative on the executive committee and was a key player in disseminating information on the status reports by placing all materials and products emanating from the subcommittees in the Reserve Book Room of the library. This avenue has been successful in that the librarian helped research and write the report and recommendations. She was also instrumental in securing additional library funding for diversity collection development and in addressing needs related to persons with disabilities. Continued success remains to be assessed as the other recommendations are implemented.

Diversity Grants: In addition to financial support from the chancellor's office, the university allocates funds for diversity grants. Over the years, librarians and the library diversity coordinator have applied for and received several grants from the chancellor, the university, and the Academic Senate. Funds have been used for collection development and outreach efforts in the form of library instruction workbooks and cultural sensitivity training workshops.

An individual grant for library instruction was used to develop and implement a peer education and training (PEAT) program for graduate students. The students were selected from different ethnic groups and disciplines and given intensive library and bibliographic instruction in exchange for their agreement to mentor undergraduate ethnic students in library research.

The first phase of the PEAT program was surprisingly successful as the graduate students were quite receptive and responsive to the skills training. An unexpected outcome of the project was the extensive networking and collaboration on research that occurred after they became familiar with major reference tools and library resources.

Phase two did not work as planned. A few of the graduate students were able to help the undergraduates with the initial workshop and overview, but because of their work schedules and the day classes of the traditional students, it became impossible to find time slots suitable for both parties. However, the positive feedback was useful for finding other ways to reinforce the library skills acquired by all participants in the program.

Diversity Trainers: As part of the university mandate, the provost provided funding to send a diverse group of faculty and administrators to a sensitivity training workshop. The library provided a representative to participate in the sessions conducted by Lee Mun Wah using his video, "Color of Fear."

Once trained, the participants were expected to return to their respective departments and help colleagues learn to be more sensitive to issues related to creating a campus climate that values different cultures. Although the goals were admirable, this project did not work well because participants felt the workshop was too generic in perspective and did not provide adequate guidance for an academic setting. Other workshop venues are being investigated for possible application to an educationally diverse environment.

Diversity Workshop Coordinator: The provost's office also received a large grant from the chancellor and funneled through the Academic Senate to fund diversity workshops in each of the six colleges and the library (as an academic unit). Funding was calculated based on full-time equivalents of students (FTEs) per department. In addition, there was an allocation for purchasing books, videos, and library materials.

Each of the departments in the six colleges was required to submit proposals for the grants. The workshops were mandated by the provost with the stipulation that all faculty be encouraged to attend. There are more than 150 departmental units; however, smaller departments were allowed to collaborate and pool resources. A committee of seven coordinators was created to draft guidelines for the proposals and topics.

Most of the departments held workshops with well-known diversity speakers. The College of Business, having received the largest allotment, sponsored a half-day workshop for the entire college and featured a panel of big-name speakers.

There were some problems with this approach and the mandate. The guidelines were not clearly stated, so many groups wanted to spend the greatest portion of the funds on food. The guidelines had to be rewritten with a percentage maximum on the food expense. Another issue involved honorariums for SJSU teaching faculty whose names were submitted to be speakers or workshop presenters. Some argued that the speakers should be non-SJSU experts, but others felt the wide diversity at SJSU made some of our faculty experts worthy of the honorariums and participation. The solution was to put a cap on the honorariums to local faculty.

The other problem worthy of mention occurred when faculty from one department chose not to participate, saying they did not perceive diversity to be an issue in their school. The provost and the committee chair met with the group on several occasions, but as there were no penalties in place for refusal to participate, there was no recourse. Because every faculty member had tenure, it was suggested that letters of reprimand be placed in their files. However, this idea was dropped because of possible conflicts with the union and faculty affairs.

In spite of the many problems associated with this initiative, the library fared quite well with its allocation. Funds were used to sponsor a diversity workshop featuring representatives from diverse student organizations on campus in a focus group format. Part of the grant was used to fund a small honorarium to the student organizations and for refreshments. The primary objective was to determine how well the library was addressing diversity from the student perspective in three major areas:

- collections;
- services;
- librarian/personnel knowledge base.

Eight student representatives were selected from more than 125 diversity-oriented student associations. Respondents provided representation from American Indian organizations (American Indian Science and Engineering Society—[AISES], and Eagle Spirit); Chicanos (M.E.C.H.A.); students with disabilities (Disabled Students Association); Asian Americans (several groups); reentry or nontraditional students; and others.

The gay and lesbian student group, which had been responsive in the past, declined the offer to participate as antigay sentiment was fairly high at the time because of the university's stand on the ROTC and its antigay policy. (The government was threatening to cancel millions in research grants and scholarship funding if the university enforced an inclusivity position that would negate the ROTC's policy.)

The student representatives polled their organizations on these three areas and came to the open forum with concrete ideas and recommendations for ways the library could improve performance and services. It was concluded that, generally, the library was doing a good job, but there were requests for more popular or current music, and ethnic titles in the magazine-browsing collection.

The Disabled Student Association even donated magazine subscriptions and a "grabber" (an instrument for reaching books on top shelves). It was a win-win situation: Library personnel were impressed with the students' familiarity with their services, and the student groups were pleased to have been consulted about issues relevant to their academic success at the university.

Aside from planning the location, contacting the student groups, and providing refreshments, this endeavor was relatively simple and easy to complete. This focus group format can be replicated with community groups for a public library or in any school with diverse student organizations. A final report with recommendations and a possible time line for implementing the suggestions may be included. Finally, a follow-up session was proposed to monitor and report on changes.

Library Diversity Initiative

The library has long been supportive of diversity and inclusion of all groups. It has implemented several initiatives to help students and patrons from different backgrounds, learning styles, and abilities/disabilities. Most of the more visible accommodations consist of taped library tours, collections in different formats, and materials or handouts in several languages. At SJSU, there is a high-technology laboratory for persons with disabilities along with adaptive technology at several computer workstations in the main library.

The university has taken a few extra steps, as have several institutions of higher learning, by creating special resource centers and by hiring persons with specific responsibilities for addressing diversity. The SJSU library hired a diversity coordinator and collaborates with four resource centers:

- Africana Research Center;
- Chicano Resource Center;
- High Tech Center for Persons with Disabilities;
- Women's Resource Center.

As the names imply, these resources centers house specialized collections and materials by and about these groups. The High Tech Center houses adaptive equipment and technology for students with disabilities. It also provides training and staff support.

Diversity Coordinator/Multicultural Services Librarian

More recently, the library has elevated the status of diversity with the hiring of a multicultural services librarian/diversity coordinator reporting to the reference department. Responsibilities for this position include active participation in state, regional, university, and library projects as well as collection development and outreach to diverse clientele in the campus community.

As part of the outreach effort, the librarian met with several of the different student organizations to make them aware of the library's collections and services and to encourage them to make book suggestions and recommendations for purchases to improve its holdings. One of the positive results of the meetings was the donation of several popular titles in Vietnamese (including a book of poetry by written by students) by the Vietnamese Student Association. Other groups donated serial subscriptions and titles for the collection.

Staff sensitivity training, customized library instruction on cultural pluralism, exhibits, and diversity projects also came under the umbrella of this position. The coordinator was also encouraged to garner support and involvement of library employees and student assistants to work on diversity projects. To achieve this support, a multicultural equity committee (MEC) composed of representatives and volunteers from each of the library and instructional resource center departments was convened.

The MEC and its subcommittees were the key players responsible for implementing a host of diversity activities for the library and the instructional resource center. The first act of the MEC was to survey library and IRC staff for their levels of understanding of other cultures and the types of activities they would be interested in attending. The survey responses led to the creation of several subcommittees. At its height, the MEC had three subcommittees of five to nine persons each that generated a large number of excellent projects including cultural enrichment and exhibits committees.

The Cultural Enrichment Committee was primarily responsible for staff cultural enrichment. Its agenda included scheduling informative videos on diverse cultures, securing guest speakers and artists, and making arrangements for luncheons at local ethnic restaurants. For restaurant outings, the committee provided menus and forms for ordering and calculating costs prior to the trip so that employees could dine within their allocated time periods. These outings were well attended by library faculty and staff.

The holistic approach to diversity assumed by this particular subcommittee entailed inviting family members and the university to their functions using flyers and announcements in the school paper. The informative videos on different countries and cultures, lectures, travel talks, and performances by ethnic artists received large audiences thanks to general interest in the subject matter and the advertising.

The Cultural Enrichment Committee also worked on several projects selected by the committee. One project the committee undertook was the creation of a cookbook. A large number of recipes was collected from the multi-ethnic workforce and compiled for printing and duplication. However, because no funding was allocated for the committee, the project had to be dropped.

An international language directory was another successful project produced by this committee. The committee compiled a list of the names and languages spoken and written by library/IRC employees and student assistants. This product had an impressive number of languages and skill levels. There were several referrals to the lists, and it was particularly useful for students interested in making themselves available for commercial translation. The directory was also useful to the acquisitions and cataloging departments in interpreting titles and making recommendations for collection development.

As its title suggests, the Exhibits Committee selected different holidays, cultural events, and issues for the exhibit and display cases. It collected books and materials, created bibliographies, and composed explanatory notes for the items and ethnic artifacts solicited from staff members for display in the locked cases.

Some of the exhibits were handled by student organizations. For example, the Muslim Student Association had an exhibit on Ramadan. The Chinese New Year, TET—Vietnamese New Year, Women's History Month, Gay and Lesbian Awareness Week (October), Cinco de Mayo, independence days for various countries, and African American Heritage Month were a few of the themes.

Collection Development

Collection development was one of the responsibilities of the multicultural services librarian. The library allocated a budget for books, videos, and journals for multicultural materials. This allotment was in addition to separate accounts for the Asian American Studies Program, the Chicano Resource Center, and the African American Studies Department.

Collection development for increasing diversity in the acquisition of materials has been greatly enhanced by the growing number of vendor catalogs on specific ethnic groups and special populations. Further, the creation and maintenance of several resource centers for different groups adds to the availability and variety of multicultural materials and references, including electronic resources such as Ethnic Newswatch on CD-Rom.

Special Assignments and Resource Centers

Some institutions have librarians or personnel to address needs of specific groups. For example, at SJSU, there is a liaison for the Disabled Student Services. There is also the diversity coordinator and various library liaisons for African American studies, Women's studies, religious studies, Asian American studies, and Chicano studies. In addition, following spirited protests and input from students, SJSU created specialized research centers for certain populations, including the Chicano Resource Center, the Africana Center, the High Tech Center (for persons with disabilities), and the Women's Resource Center.

Library Instruction & Research Guides

As was noted by Ellen Broidy (1988) at the sixteenth annual LOEX conference, library and bibliographic instructors must celebrate diversity by teaching library skills as if people mattered. In keeping with this perspective, library bibliographers have created research guides that emphasize diversity. There are specialized handouts on cultural pluralism, religion, and ethnic-specific groups such as African Americans, Asians, and Asians in America.

Other bibliographers have incorporated diversity into broader subject areas. For example, the health sciences bibliographer has resource materials on health and culture to direct researchers to works emphasizing the importance of culture and anthropological underpinnings of ritual in the health and healing process.

Library and bibliographic instruction is customized to incorporate diversity into the presentations and sessions. The library is also actively involved in a large number of summer programs sponsored by the university for different underrepresented groups. Examples and library exercises can be tailored to entice these populations to engage in scholarly research with clever assignments such as comparative analyses of rap music with other types of music and periods of music history. Or for a health sciences class, the librarian can design exercises emphasizing research on juvenile diabetes, Tay Sachs, sickle-cell anemia, fetal alcohol syndrome, or other diseases that are more prevalent in certain ethnic groups. By personalizing the search topic, diverse student groups can be motivated to engage in more scholarly research.

Sharing information with colleagues and teaching faculty is equally important. To achieve this goal, presentations featuring new databases and resources, such as Ethnic Newswatch, are made during regularly scheduled reference department meetings to librarians and to teaching faculty at their departmental meetings. It should be noted that most librarians are liaisons and regularly attend departmental meetings in their respective subject areas. Attendance at these meetings increases their visibility.

Focus Groups and Open Forums

As previously mentioned, the library received funding from the university diversity grant and workshop program and the library diversity coordinator conducted an open forum in which students representatives from the 125 diverse student organizations on campus were invited to attend a session with all library personnel. These types of forums can be easily tailored to meet the needs of other libraries and groups.

Specific Events

Certain holidays and events lend themselves to library support and involvement. Acknowledgment of the following holidays can be done with minimal effort and staff involvement. Most of the holidays can be joint sponsorships with the respective faculty and staff associations, and the student groups. Some of the following events have been acknowledged with the associated activity:

African American Events

• **Juneteenth** (June 13–19): To commemorate jubilation and freedom in 1865 when slaves in the westernmost states received news of the Emancipation Proclamation. A few books are available for use in exhibits, but reading lists and library presence at the outdoor festivals are a good start.

• **Kwanzaa** (December 26–31): Joint sponsorship of ceremonies with community organizations, bibliographies, exhibits of books, and explanations of the primary symbols such as:

~ Mkeka (straw mat);
~ Kinara (candle holder that holds seven candles);
~ Mshumaa (seven candles representing Seven Principles);
~ Muhindi (ear of corn representing offspring or product);
~ Kikombe Cha Umoja (unity cup for libations);
~ Zawadi (gifts symbolizing fruits of the labor);
~ Karamu (the feast for which there are recipe books).

In addition, there are explanations of Nguzo Saba, or the seven principles, which include umoja (unity), kujichagulia (self-determination), ujima (collective work and responsibility), ujamaa (cooperative economics), nia (purpose), kuumba (creativity), and imani (faith). Joint sponsors have included employee and student organizations and community groups such as local churches and social groups. The booklists and recipes of Kwanzaa dishes also work well for handouts and brochures. Ethnic cuisine and the feasts are equally inviting avenues for distributing informative pamphlets.

Asian American Events

• **Chinese New Year**: Joint sponsorship of activities with the Asian American Faculty and Staff Association and student organizations.

• **TET Festival/Vietnamese New Year**: Joint sponsorship, exhibits, booths at the local festivals, and assistance with the publicity by distributing posters and flyers.

Chicano Events

As with the other ethnic groups, Cinco de Mayo, the Day of the Dead, Mexican Independence Day, La Raza, and other special days can be used to acknowledge the culture using books, art, and exhibits.

Political and Historical Issues

A unique holocaust exhibit consisting of six million slivers representing the number of Jews killed created an informative display for the library. Likewise, an array of art and sculpture consisting of a white fist clenching barbed wire was used to commemorate the Treaty of Guadualupe Hidalgo and to portray the U.S. treatment of indigenous Mexicans. Both exhibits generated lively discussion and debate.

Religious Groups
Events such as Ramadan and groups such as the Islamic Student Association have had displays on exhibit at the library. Booklets and pamphlets explaining their beliefs and practices have been well received.

Travels and Tourism
The university often hosts international guests visiting Silicon Valley for technology training and development. Following a trip to Thailand by library technology trainers, the library was able to prepare an exhibit of Thai souvenirs (maps, silk ties and trinkets, dolls) and books. The group of Thai librarians and educators was pleasantly surprised to see symbols of their homeland during their training sessions in San Jose and at the university.

Women's History Month
The library can sponsor authors' teas and book talks featuring local female authors. Exhibits of the achievements and inventions of women can be used in display cases, along with bibliographies.

Other Possibilities
Many other ethnic, religious, and seasonal observations lend themselves to diversity celebrations and collaborative sponsorship. A few of the more popular events include:

Ethnic/Status Celebrations
- African American Heritage Month
- Asian American Heritage Month
- Cinco de Mayo
- Chinese New Year
- Gay and Lesbian Awareness Week
- Hispanic Heritage Month
- Kwaanza
- Native American Heritage Month
- TET—Vietnamese New Year
- Womens' History Month

Religious Observations
- Jewish New Year
- Ramadan
- Rosh Hashanah and the Day of Judgment
- Yom Kippur

Seasonal
- Chinese Annual Moon Festival
- Green Corn Festival

The diverse student enrollment has provided other unique opportunities for librarians to promote cultural enrichment. For example, the university sponsors the general convocation for the whole campus followed by college and departmental ceremonies. Because some of our students of color are the first college graduates in their families, it was decided there should be another avenue for family and friends to participate in the pomp and grandeur. The solution was to have a Black Graduation and a Chicano Commencement acknowledging the academic achievements of graduates from these respective ethnic groups.

Library personnel (faculty as well as staff) have been involved in these activities, although not serving in a traditional librarian mode. They have been on the subcommittees to read essays submitted by students vying to be the "student speaker" (as opposed to a valedictorian) for the ceremony. They have also helped in the planning process, editing the program with appropriate program acknowledgments to library personnel for their assistance and support, and with commendations during the actual ceremony.

Conclusion

In summary, the opportunities for promoting diversity in library and library affiliates are unlimited. With proper planning and inclusion of key actors and support groups, any library can engage in productive activities or sponsor events that include all segments of society. The rewards are equally limitless for efforts made and successfully implemented functions and programs. The planners and participants need only have open minds and be willing to be innovative and inclusive.

References

Alire, Camila. 1997a. Ethnic populations: A model for statewide services. *American Libraries* 28(10):38–40.

———. 1997b. Mentoring on my mind: It takes a family to graduate a minority library professional. *American Libraries* 28(10):41.

Broidy, Ellen. 1988. Celebrating Diversity: Teaching library skills as if people mattered. In *Reaching and Teaching Diverse Library Users*, ed. Teresa Mensching. Ann Arbor, Mich.: Pierian Press.

Horner, Edith. ed. 1998. *California Cities, Towns, & Counties: Basic Data Profiles for all Municipalities & Counties*. Palo, Alto, Calif.: Information Publications.

National LOEX Library Instruction Conference. 1988. *Reaching and Teaching Diverse Library Users*, Ann Arbor, Mich.: Pierian Press. ed. Teresa B. Mensching.

On Campus. 1997. San Jose, Calif.: San Jose State University Office of Public Affairs.

Riggs, Donald, and Patricia Tarin, eds. 1994. *Cultural Diversity in Libraries*. New York: Neal-Schuman.

Rosen et al. 1994. Student employees and the academic library's multicultural mission. In *Racial and Ethnic Diversity in Academic Libraries: Multicultural Issues*. Ed. Deborah Curry, Susan G. Bundy, and Lynne Martin. New York. Haworth Press.

Webster's Ninth New Collegiate Dictionary. 1988. Springfield, Mass.: Merriam-Webster.

Muses, Mind-sets, and Models:
How Technology Is Shaping Library Services

Elizabeth A. Dupuis

> Regardless of how strongly we want to cling to our better ways of
> finding information, if we fail to create the sort of library tools that
> today's students want, someone else will produce them. The re-
> sult will be that the library will increasingly become the source of
> last resort, rather than the first.
>
> ~ Martin Raish

Colleges and universities are under great pressure to prove their educational worth in today's market, to create skilled, qualified employees, and
to offer students socially and intellectually enriching experiences. In an era
of accelerated actions and consequences, academia's standard operating procedures are no longer agile enough to respond to the needs of its customers.
As a member of the higher education community, the academic library is
also challenged to prove its value and substantiate its contribution to student success. To provide meaningful services for students, librarians must
be cognizant of general societal trends as well as trends specifically affecting
today's college students.

Technology has been one of the major environmental factors in these
students' lives, shaping them as they develop and affecting the future of
industry, invention, and social policy. Like amphibians, which are considered to be sentinel species that detect environmental changes early, children may be similar harbingers of our future. By watching their actions and
responses to the world around them, we may all learn new ways to adapt.
Indeed, we should look upon students as our muses—our inspiration to
respond positively to the challenges posed by new technologies, new econo-
mies, and new business models. Adaptation will require librarians to con-
front their initial reactions and question their assumptions, to construct a
new mind-set that preserves the best of our traditional mission with the
realities of our technological environment. Many academic libraries have
already initiated noteworthy projects that embrace the philosophies of this
new mind-set, sometimes translating traditional services and occasionally
developing new models.

Students: Our Muses
Born in the 1980s, today's typical college students grew up in a technology-
saturated environment. Their childhood years of curiosity and experimentation coincided with the ingression of computers and video games in most

American homes. Equipped today with e-mail addresses, pagers, personal digital assistants, and cellular phones, college students are extremely wired and never far from the latest technological rage. Stories abound of students ripping and swapping MP3 files, playing Nintendo and PlayStation for hours, auctioning collectibles from multiplayer online games, and trading stocks online. As high school students, a surprising number started their own companies; instead of delivering papers, sacking groceries, or mowing lawns, they successfully created business plans, developed Web sites, established secure e-commerce, hired personnel, and marketed products. Overcoming challenging tasks and facing real consequences, many freshmen have already experienced the excitement and satisfaction of true problem-based learning.

These experiences are only a small portrait of how college students and younger generations have integrated technology into their lives. Recent brain research has concluded that the constant presence of technology in young adults' lives may actually cause their brains to be wired differently from previous generations. "Neuronal connections that underlie cognitive and other abilities stick around if they're used, but wither if they're not....'Teens thus have the power to determine their own brain development, to determine which connections survive and which don't', says [Jay] Giedd [of the National Institute of Mental Health]" (Begley 2000, 58–59). Adaptation to technology may be the newest chapter in the theory of survival of the fittest. Market researchers have frequently studied children as a target audience, but other companies are taking this transformation seriously as well. Microsoft, for example, recently hired two teenage consultants to provide insight into how their peers use and relate to technology (Martinez 2000).

Adam Rifkin (1998) and Don Tapscott (1998) offer two of the best starting points for understanding the attitudes of today's youth. They and other sources describe people between the ages of ten and thirty as curious, innovative, contrary, hedonistic, self-reliant, responsible, and natural multitaskers. They have grown up in schools that encouraged collaboration as much as, if not more than, competition. They expect transparent and immediate connections between themselves and other people and information. Because of their comfort with technology, they have been placed in roles of authority at young ages and some express little need for a college degree. They readily challenge assumptions and are comfortable experimenting without rules or guidelines. Their propensity for all things technological in an era dubbed the Information Age gives this generation the ability to radically change their models for learning, working, playing, and living.

Prospective students have higher expectations for the technological services offered by colleges and universities than in previous decades. Many high school students determine collegiate selections based on their initial reactions to the design and quality of information provided on the university or college Web site. By perceptively culling information from these sites, prospective students can get a feel for the culture at a particular school. Faculty and students often offer glimpses of their personal and academic interests on individual Web pages. In some ways, this type of orientation may be more informative than the traditional campus visit. Levels of technological sophistication such as high bandwidth connectivity, distance education classes, and access to online services are factors they evaluate. The *Yahoo! Internet Life* 100 Most Wired Campuses survey (Bernstein, Caplan, and Glover 2000) found that:

- Ninety-eight percent allow prospective students to apply electronically.
- Sixty-eight percent offer Web-based registration.
- Fifty-nine percent provide eight-plus hours of tech support, seven days a week.
- Forty-one percent offer some wireless access on campus.
- Thirty-eight percent offer students more than 25MB of server disk space.
- Thirty-five percent provide public computer equipment or labs in all dormitories.
- Eleven percent require students to own computers.

Arriving on campus, new college students face the immediate and timeless demands related to living arrangements, new relationships, busy schedules, academic pressures, and new freedoms. Although their academic lives are often focused on short-term goals such as finishing an assignment, studying for an exam, or getting a good grade, upon graduation they tend to take a more holistic view of their educational experiences. Students interviewed about the aspects of their alma mater that they would most like to change mentioned reducing bureaucracy, building campus cohesion and ending divisiveness, treating students with respect, and improving interactions between faculty and students. The most valuable benefits of their academic experiences included increased credibility and respect, strong friendships, fresh intellectual and social perspectives, increased social and personal confidence, and a foundation for future self-education (Greene 1998). Though information literacy and technology skills were not specifically mentioned, they add inherent value to many of these broader benefits of the college experience.

Libraries: A New Mind-set

With the proliferation of technologies and nearly ubiquitous public access to the Internet, academic librarians are unsettled by questions such as What is the future for library services when students have access to information without need of intermediaries? Without recounting the predictions of many would-be futurists, let us simply consider students' perceptions and expectations of libraries.

Most college students have formulated their definition of a library based on their experiences as children. Many students were introduced at young ages to school and public libraries that emphasized reading programs and basic research skills. Although the presence of new technologies is not necessarily an indicator of quality resources, institutions that have not integrated technology are likely to be seen by younger generations as mausoleums managed by out-of-touch staff. A survey about the future of public libraries states, "the youngest Americans polled, those between the ages of 18 and 24, are the least enthusiastic boosters of maintaining and building library buildings. They are also the least enthusiastic of any age group about the importance of libraries in a digital future....While only a fifth of respondents said they thought libraries would become less important in the digital age, those with access to computers were most likely to feel this way" (Benton Foundation 1996). However, librarians often reiterate that familiarity with computers or technology does not necessarily imply comprehension of, or adeptness with, information skills. Not surprisingly, one study of incoming college students confirmed that there is little correlation between a student's high self-confidence in his or her ability to do library research and his or her knowledge of library concepts (Geffert and Christensen 1998).

It is probable that most public service librarians have heard at least one thankful student lament, "I didn't know about these resources or search strategies earlier." Yet, it remains unclear exactly why so many college students avoid the library until the last minute, if not altogether. Some possible reasons might be that:

- Library collections are overwhelming in their size and organization.
- Faculty do not create assignments that draw on the richness of the collections.
- The Internet offers enough content to meet most undergraduate needs.
- Library systems do not adequately meet students' academic and personal needs.
- Students are simply not aware of what they are overlooking.

When reconsidering how academic libraries can help students succeed, answers should come from honest assessments of student needs and creative uses of technology to redesign problematic services and fill voids where services are absent altogether.

Without question, the Internet has changed how all types of organizations manage their internal work and communicate with their customers. The marketplace is capitalizing on the knowledge economy as technology is creating faster, more convenient ways to access some types of information. Many new competitors are emerging for all industries.

It has been almost universally true that established players were not the leaders in taking advantage of new technology.... Newcomers, unbur-

dened by tradition, overheads, and old expectations, have usually been
the ones to take over. That is the danger facing libraries....What these
new players do may not fit the traditional requirements that librarians
would have insisted on, but it may be sufficient and even more appropriate for a new medium (Odlyzko 1997, 161).

New businesses and enterprising individuals have begun marketing
librarylike services to individuals (Kotlas 1998). For example, information
brokers contract to research and prioritize findings, publishers sell portions
of publications to consumers directly, Internet service providers and cable
companies provide customers access to article databases from home, book-
stores encourage browsing for books online, and document couriers deliver information to doorsteps or desktops. It has yet to be determined if
these companies will survive in the long term, but their presence pushes
libraries to acknowledge that the systems have changed. Because libraries
cannot thrive—or even survive—by avoiding the market, they must adapt
to it and participate in it. Sources that discuss general applications of, and
policies related to, technology, such as the online journal *First Monday* (First
Monday 2000), are relevant to libraries as well. Our competition and colleagues are also operating in this electronic environment, so we can easily
watch and learn from their successes and failures as much as they can learn
from ours.

Certainly, computers and technologies have already helped libraries
reach beyond their walls to extend their services, but to transition to the
digital environment, librarians cannot simply map traditional services to a
Web context and consider their work successful. There must be a fundamental reassessment of their approaches and services. Libraries can no longer
accept antiquated and disjointed systems from their own institutions or from
the companies with which they negotiate. Inadequacies of current electronic resources to which libraries subscribe reflect poorly on the library
rather than on the vendor. To better serve all library patrons, librarians must
evolve from the current role of continually explaining systems to users to a
new role as advocate for more intuitive interfaces and more sophisticated
infrastructures between systems. Librarians might also consider that most
undergraduates are simply looking for good information—not the best information or the most comprehensive information—just some relevant information on a topic. From this perspective, a quick search for recent full-
text articles or Web pages may be a satisfactory approach. In the near future,
the librarian's role may shift from information curator to information counselor, mentoring people through the process of selecting and evaluating the
data they need.

Just as instruction librarians have shifted from a preference for teacher-
centered to student-centered learning, library services overall may be shifting from library controlled to library moderated. Many libraries are already

considering new delivery systems, new information management models, and new communication mechanisms. Distilling the sentiments expressed in many technology circles, it would be prudent for libraries to consider features such as:

• *Convenience*: Expectations for all types of services have risen. People want easy access and immediate responses. Libraries should strive to provide as much real-time, online service as possible. As other companies and members of the university community fill the demands "anytime, anyplace" so too should libraries. Systems and services should be seamlessly integrated.

• *Personalization*: Services should be customizable for individuals and even flexible to each person's changing needs or interests. Students want the ability to determine the manner with which they request services and the level of information or explanation they receive. Tailoring services also allows libraries to create and satisfy niche markets within the university and perhaps even develop different levels of fee-based services to accommodate varying personal styles.

• *Collaboration*: Growing numbers of online resources focus on the creation of community. By nature, universities already have a community of students whether they are on or off campus. New resources should provide mechanisms for communication between novice and novice, novice and expert, and expert and expert within academia. Resources that can be utilized by groups within the institution and by other institutions are equally valuable.

Technology: Models of Library Services

Many academic libraries have developed notable projects and services that illustrate some of these new methods of delivery, management, and communication. Some of these examples mimic traditional services; others create new models of service or access. By nature, most of these services utilize technology in ways that serve traditional on-campus students, as well as students in distance education programs and other members of the academic community.

Computing Facilities

A number of campuses host large computing labs within their libraries. The best of these facilities provide access to network connections, software applications, varied work spaces, and expertise. The Information Arcade at the University of Iowa's main library (University of Iowa 2000), the Information Commons at the University of Southern California's Leavey Library (University of Southern California 2000), and the Knapp Media and Technology Center at Wellesley College (Wellesley College 2000) are three examples of academic libraries that offer a full range of computing equipment and work spaces within their facilities. Besides the standard productivity applications and network resources, these libraries also offer wired group study rooms for collaborative projects, hands-on classrooms, audio-video creation and editing stations, scanners, and digital cameras. Students and faculty have access to assistance from teams of librarians, computing staff, and writing consultants. Many of these facilities are self-service with automated log-ins and direct billing for any printing. In these environments students can easily participate as consumers and producers of information in a variety of formats.

Network Ports and Wireless Services

Many campuses are shifting support away from large campus computer labs and, instead, are mandating that freshmen arrive on campus with a personal computer or laptop. One of the benefits of this shift is the option of providing access to the Internet in more creative and flexible ways. A number of libraries around the country have installed laptop ports at every study seat in the library. Alternately, some schools are experimenting with wireless services for laptops and portable devices. Carnegie Mellon University has received recognition for implementing a campuswide wireless network called Wireless Andrew and a complementary initiative called Handheld Andrew (Carnegie Mellon 2000). As computing devices get smaller, libraries and other campus agencies will have to provide more access in more accommodating ways.

Smart Cards

One oft-discussed type of technology is the smart card, or one card, which can be used as a multipurpose university identification card, housing key, and debit card. Information about registration, library circulation records, athletic tickets, dining, banking, and authorized access to buildings would all be saved onto a computer chip embedded within an ID the size of a credit card. Concerns about monopolistic systems and privacy are weighted against the benefits of having one integrated and personalized system for student and faculty affairs. Libraries often use smart cards to allow access to buildings during evening hours and to check out library materials to borrowers. The University of New Mexico has implemented a version of this technology (Gallagher 1999).

Web Sites

Although some students will naturally gravitate to a campus library, many others will prefer using the Web for research. Most academic libraries have a Web site, though it is disturbing to note that many colleges and universities do not have an obvious link to it from their campus home page. On servers managed by the library or campus computing department, academic library Web pages often include hours, location, library-related news and events, descriptions of their departments and services, links to search engines, and lists of other reference tools (Cohen and Still 1999). As our understanding of Web page design has evolved, there is growing support for viewing the Web site not simply as a guide to the physical library, but also as a resource unto itself. Certainly for distance education students, but also for on-campus students who choose to do their research from their residence hall or computer lab, the library's Web site should provide sufficient organization, content, and assistance.

Adaptive Technology

Blind and physically disabled students use adaptive technologies to access resources from the electronic library and the Internet. On most campuses, they will find the hardware and software they need within the library. Although all electronic resources, including Web sites, should meet the Americans with Disabilities Act (ADA) and World Wide Web Consortium (W3C) accessibility standards, many do not. The Equal Access to Software and Information site, hosted by the Rochester Institute of Technology, provides more information about issues and advancements in the field (Rochester Institute of Technology 2000).

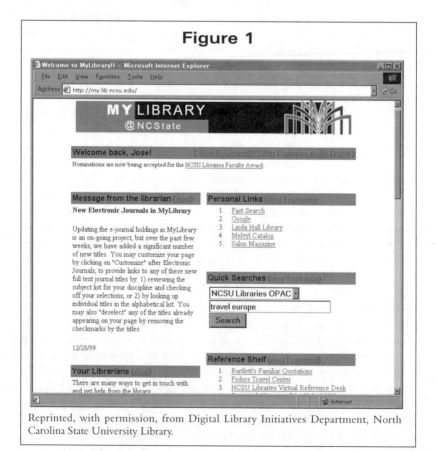

Figure 1

Reprinted, with permission, from Digital Library Initiatives Department, North Carolina State University Library.

Portals

Portals are currently a popular approach to collecting and organizing resources relevant to a particular group of people. Many portals focus on an audience based on hobbies, age, or profession. Some libraries are applying this principle of personalization to their Web sites. (See figure 1.) The Digital Library Initiatives Department in the North Carolina State University Library has developed MyLibrary@NCState, which allows individuals at their university to create a customized interface to library resources of interest to them (North Carolina State 1999). MyLibrary pages are collections of links relevant to and chosen by an individual. Students or faculty members simply log on, create a profile, select the items most relevant to their academic or personal research, and save their selections, which they can re-edit at any time. Once created, the tailored pages also offer reminders about due dates for library materials, announcements about new books related to their interests, and messages from librarians in their discipline. Other libraries, such as Virginia Commonwealth University, Cornell University, and California Polytechnic State University, have also developed variations of MyLibrary-type sites. Recently, a group of twenty-four colleges and universities partnered to develop generic portal software; the source code will be available to any other interested college (Olsen 2000a).

Online Catalogs

Today, most academic libraries have online catalogs, many of which are Web based, allowing patrons to search for items without learning special commands. In addition, Web-based catalogs integrate records for print materials, electronic materials subscribed to by the library, and free Web sites recommended by subject specialists. Some online catalogs offer online renewals, electronic holds, and even requests to page and deliver items to an office. Though perhaps a time-consuming process, to those online catalogs libraries could add tables of contents for all books, as well as links to book reviews. Amazon.com is an obvious example of some of these services (Amazon.com 2000). Rated lists of the best books or best Web sites might no longer be limited to national boards and close circles of friends; today's technologies allow people, rather than computers, to judge the quality of items and make recommendations to a shared database. This type of collaborative filtering allows people to find items endorsed by people with similar interests, and its validity would be compounded by its continued use over time. The University of Minnesota, the University of California at Berkeley, and the Massachusetts Institute of Technology are currently experimenting with this technique.

Circulation Services

The types of materials, and the manner in which they can be borrowed, have also changed. As students gain longer hours of access to the building and the use of the online catalog, it is reasonable for them to want to borrow materials later in the evening as well. A number of colleges and universities offer stations for students to check out books or videos to themselves with a simple scanning machine and receipt system. In addition, some libraries have extended the types of materials that can be checked out from their staffed desks to include laptops, digital cameras, and scanners. The new lending policies have also added new check-in procedures to ensure that materials are still functioning and ready for the next borrower.

Proxy Services

Access to the collection outside the library and off-campus is of growing interest as more campuses install ports in residence hall rooms and support larger numbers of distance education students. Authorization and authentication can be provided through methods such as proxy servers and digital certificates. A proxy server is a networked computer that acts as an intermediary between a user's computer and a remote server, authorizing online users to access restricted or licensed resources. Configuring a browser for a proxy server is fairly simple, though negotiating with publishers and managing many subnets can be more complex.

Digital Certificates

Another technology gaining recent press is the digital certificate, an electronic identifier issued by a third party, called a certificate authority, which validates the identity of a person through a cryptographic system.

> The most common form of digital certificates are signature certificates, which contain some base information (typically name, organization, location, and often e-mail address), a public key, and a digital signature. The public key is used to verify the signature, and the signature is used to verify that the certificate is valid and has not been altered. When you request a signature certificate, a public/private key pair is generated and the base information is sent to the [certificate authority]. The [certificate authority] then generates the certificate, signs the public key (with the certificate authority's private key), and sends it back to the requester (Pleas 1999, 203).

The public and private keys are all codes that allow both sender and recipient to ensure the integrity of the content they are sharing and to verify each other's identities. The certificate authority vouches for the authenticity of each of the parties after they present this electronic information. The Center for Research in Educational Networking (CREN) and the Massachusetts Institute of Technology have launched a Certificate Authority Service (Center for Research 2000). To ensure secure transactions and resource sharing over the Internet, this service reviews, validates, and issues digital certificates. It also verifies the authenticity and integrity of the documents themselves. The University of Pittsburgh has already issued thousands of digital certificates to their students and staff to make purchases at school stores and to conduct other university business (Olsen 2000b). It is possible that digital certificates will evolve into the most common form of authorization and authentication for colleges and universities within the next few years.

Electronic Reserves

Historically, academic libraries have partnered with faculty to offer reserve services for students. Faculty could place complete texts, copies of individual articles, and homework answers or old exams on reserve as resources for their classes. These traditional services moved to an online environment in the late 1980s. Electronic reserves are now one of the most popular services with students, allowing them—usually from password-protected Web sites—to access supplementary materials at hours most convenient for them. One notable example is ERes at San Diego State University, a Web-based electronic reserve system offering access to course readings, links to electronic databases, course bulletin boards, and chat rooms (San Diego State 2000). Electronic reserves can also offer new media; for example, the Bobst Library at New York University hosts audio- and video-streaming reserves, including many for foreign language courses (New York University 1999).

Electronic Books and Electronic Journals

Electronic books, including those of public domain texts provided by Project Gutenberg (Project Gutenberg and Promo.net 2000), have risen in popularity as people experiment with portable devices that display texts. Subscription companies such as netLibrary allow patrons to preview, read, check out, and download electronic books (published materials in digital form) from a collection. These services often tout new features such as the ability to do full-text searches of entire books. Electronic journals from subscription services such as JSTOR and Science Direct allow students to search for articles and view or save them in HTML and PDF formats. As costs of books and periodical subscriptions rise, libraries must continually make collection development decisions based on cost, format, and convenience. One radical approach was instituted by the library director at Stevens Institute of Technology, who cancelled all paper subscriptions to research-oriented periodicals and, instead, supplied all information to faculty and students via electronic services on demand (Widdicombe 1994–1995).

Periodical Databases

Electronic periodical databases are provided to students through either individual library subscriptions or consortia agreements. Some databases merely provide citations and abstracts; others offer full text or full content. For libraries with subscriptions to numerous databases, certain periodical titles are indexed by a variety of databases, but each database may cover different dates or offer different levels of content. Ideally, a student would be able to conduct a search simultaneously across all databases available in the library, reduce duplicates, remove items not available within their library system, and effortlessly determine the URL or library location to retrieve the item. Although this type of integrated system does not currently exist, JAKE provides an interesting first step toward this end. JAKE (Jointly Administered Knowledge Environment), developed at the Cushing/Whitney Medical Library at the Yale University School of Medicine, is a useful resource for cross-referencing lists of journal titles and issues indexed in databases and distinguishing between those provided as citations only and those with full text (Yale University 2000). The information can be localized to include only those resources and holdings owned by a specific institution's library. JAKE is notable not only for its value as a collection development tool, but also because of its intent to create a repository of information about electronic sources that can be added to and used by any interested library.

Printing and Document Delivery

Many institutions ceased offering free printing and initiated printing services for which charges are debited from a copy card or smart card. At some schools, students on the campus network can choose to send print jobs from remote locations to the printers in the computing labs to pick up when they are again on campus. This service offers students an easy mechanism for regular, color, and transparency printouts. Cost recovery mechanisms support not only the expenses for paper, but also the subscription services from which students often print articles. For those resources not available in the library, interlibrary loan departments have traditionally offered to request items from other institutions. Today, some departments are offering new document delivery options where students can request any item not available online in full text. Staff will retrieve, copy, and deliver the item for a slightly higher fee than charged in the past.

Digital Libraries

Many academic libraries are digitizing unique aspects of their own collections such as photographs, manuscripts, rare books, maps, recorded sound, and moving pictures. Some of these digitization projects are affiliated with the Digital Libraries Initiative (Library of Congress 1999), sponsored by the Library of Congress; others are localized to their own campus. In addition, a few libraries have begun to offer services for collecting and organizing large digital collections of information created by members of their own academic community. One example is the Networked Digital Library of Theses and Dissertations, a project initiated by Virginia Tech that has attracted approximately ninety other institutional members (Networked Digital Library 2000). The digital dissertation project is a model for libraries offering indexing, searching, and information architecture services to organize, access, and archive a range of publications and data sets for their institution.

Subject Guides

To assist patrons in selecting the best resources in certain fields, libraries provide subject guides or pathfinders. As a first step, paper handouts were turned into Web pages or PDF files for students to view from the Web site. In a new incarnation, SourceFinder (Virginia Military Institute 2000) and Data Genie (California Polytechnic 2000), developed by the Virginia Military Institute Library and California Polytechnic State University, San Luis Obispo, respectively, offer wonderful examples of subject guides created on the fly for researchers. (See figure 2.) Students and faculty have the ability to customize the information they retrieve. The layout remains consistent, and the resources are easy for library staff to maintain. Each site displays subject resources based on variables such as type of sources needed, format of information, and restrictions on research time. Although many libraries offer subject guides, few use the technology to dynamically generate a list of only those sources most relevant to the researcher's current needs.

Electronic Reference

Reference services can be provided creatively to meet the demands for longer hours and more customized assistance. Many libraries now provide reference services via e-mail or chat, often called "Ask a Librarian." Though some libraries have restrictive policies about the number of requests permitted and the types of questions answered, the services are likely to rise in popularity as more students focus on using the resources available remotely. One example of this type of reference service is the Virtual Reference Desk Project, based at Syracuse University and sponsored by the ERIC Clearinghouse on Information & Technology, the United States Department of Education's National Library of Education, and the White House Office of Science & Technology Policy (Virtual Reference Desk Project 2000). This project models the provision of seamless, human-mediated, Internet-based reference services. Answers are provided by a variety of subject experts in geographically disparate regions to more than fifty million K–12 students, parents, and educators. People with subject expertise can volunteer to participate in the provision of reference services by joining the Ask a Consortium. Sponsored by the Library of Congress and piloted in 2000, a similar project called Collaborative Digital Reference Service provides high-quality online reference service through an international collaboration of corporate, public, national, and academic libraries to any patron regardless of age, nationality, or affiliation (Library of Congress 2000).

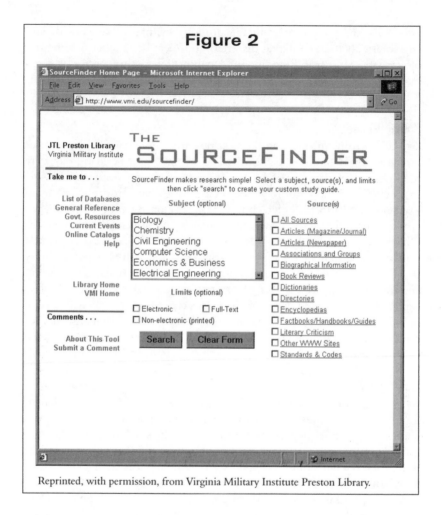

Figure 2

Reprinted, with permission, from Virginia Military Institute Preston Library.

Library Instruction Programs

For many years, library instruction classes have focused on search strategies for finding articles or books using CD-ROM databases and online catalogs. More recently, students have been turning to the Internet to begin their research. In response, library instruction classes have incorporated more information about evaluation skills, plagiarism, and the differences between resources. Lecture- and demonstration-style classes have given way to active and collaborative learning techniques in hands-on classrooms. Many academic libraries offer free workshops to the university community and public on topics ranging from general library sources to advanced Web publishing. Occasional workshops and course-integrated classes are evolving into more formalized programs, such as new learning communities and information literacy programs. A number of years ago, new learning communities began striking partnerships among librarians, instructional designers, information technologists, and other campus experts to blend information and technology with curricular content. Successful programs were modeled at a number of schools, including Indiana University-Purdue University Indianapolis and California Polytechnic State University, San Luis Obispo. Other libraries have developed similar information literacy programs. Information literacy programs generally create partnerships between librarians and faculty to infuse a progression of skills to search, select, and evaluate information. These programs are often implemented as stand-alone, credit-bearing courses or segments within courses of many other departments at the university (Grassian and Clark 1999).

Figure 3

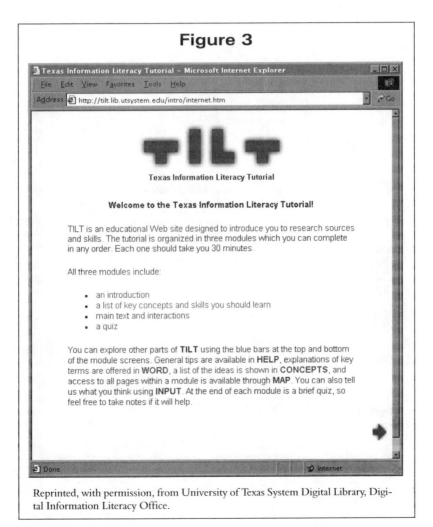

Reprinted, with permission, from University of Texas System Digital Library, Digital Information Literacy Office.

Online Tutorials

There are many possible approaches to teaching information and research skills, though the current trend is to develop online tutorials for students. (See figure 3.) Developed by the Digital Information Literacy Office for the University of Texas System, TILT is one example (University of Texas 2000). TILT is a Web-based, self-paced educational site designed to teach undergraduates fundamental research skills in a series of three modules. Students learn to select appropriate sources for research, to search library databases and Internet search engines effectively, and to evaluate and cite both print and online information. Throughout the tutorial are interactions, which are designed to allow the students to practice applying the concepts discussed. Each module takes approximately thirty minutes to complete and concludes

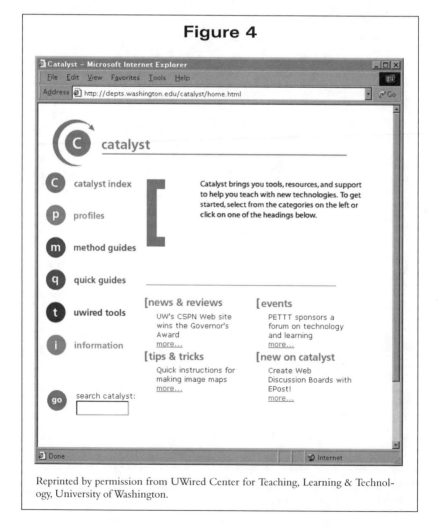

Figure 4

Reprinted by permission from UWired Center for Teaching, Learning & Technology, University of Washington.

with a quiz that offers students immediate feedback. TILT is cross-browser and cross-platform compatible and available to students anywhere.

Faculty Instructional Support

Librarians on many campuses also provide services to support faculty such as consulting on appropriate library-related assignments and providing information about online teaching and learning techniques. As faculty are more forcefully encouraged to transfer their classes to an online environment, instructional support from agencies such as the library grow increasingly necessary. For such a purpose, UWired at the University of Washington developed Catalyst (University of Washington 1999). (See Figure 4.) Catalyst provides faculty with the information to select and develop high-quality instructional materials online. The site includes profiles of educators, examples of best practices, recommendations for sound pedagogical practice, detailed technical support, and course Web page templates. This project builds a community and allows educators to share ideas with—and learn from—their peers.

Summary

The abundance of information resources and the public's increased comfort with technology emphasizes the need for libraries to change the perception of what their institutions offer, as well as to earnestly reassess the services the libraries support. Students do seek out campus resources that address their needs. Academic libraries can best promote themselves as one of these resources if they offer services that build on this generation's preference for adaptability, experimentation, expediency, independence, and collaboration. Library philosophies are already evolving from "just in case" to "just in time" and now "just for me" (Raish 2000). Although no one can predict the future with certainty, experimenting with these new services gives librarians a chance not only to better understand the technological world but to participate in shaping it as well.

References

Amazon.com, Inc. 2000. Amazon.com [cited 1 May 2000]. Available from http://www.amazon.com/; INTERNET.

Begley, Sharon. 2000. Getting inside a teen brain. *Newsweek* 135 (28 February):58–59 [cited 1 May 2000]. Available from Expanded Academic ASAP, <http://infotrac.galegroup.com/>.

Benton Foundation. 1996. *Buildings, Books, and Bytes: Libraries and Communities in the Digital Age* [cited 1 May 2000]. Available from http://www.benton.org/Library/Kellogg/summary.html; INTERNET.

Bernstein, Rob, Jeremy Caplan, and Eric Glover. 2000. America's Most Wired Colleges 2000. *Yahoo! Internet Life* [cited 30 April 2000]. Available from http://www.zdnet.com/yil/content/college/; INTERNET.

California Polytechnic State University, San Luis Obispo. 2000. *The Data Genie* [cited 1 May 2000]. Available from http://www.lib.calpoly.edu/research/ data_genie.html; INTERNET.

Carnegie Mellon University. 2000. *Carnegie Mellon Introduces Wireless Network* [cited 1 May 2000]. Available from http://www.cmu.edu/home/news/wireless.html; INTERNET.

Center for Research in Educational Computing. 2000. *CREN's Certificate Authority Service* [cited 30 April 2000]. Available from http://www.cren.net/ca/; INTERNET.

Cohen, Laura B., and Julie M. Still. 1999. A comparison of research university and two-year college library Web sites: Content, functionality, and form. *College & Research Libraries* 60:275–89 [cited 1 May 2000]. Available from Periodical Abstracts, <http://www.texshare.edu/ovidweb/ovidweb.cgi>.

First Monday. 2000. *First Monday: Peer Reviewed Journal on the Internet* [cited 1 May 2000]. Available from http://www.firstmonday.dk/; INTERNET.

Gallagher, Joe. 1999. Accessing the campus. American School & University. 71:66–71B [cited 6 June 2000]. Available from Expanded Academic ASAP, <http://infotrac.galegroup.com/>.

Geffert, Bryn, and Beth Christensen. 1998. Things they carry. *Reference & User Services Quarterly* 37:279–89 [cited 1 May 2000]. Available from Periodical Abstracts, <http://www.texshare.edu/ovidweb/ovidweb.cgi>.

Grassian, Esther, and Susan E. Clark. 1999. Information literacy sites: Background and ideas for program planning and development. *College and Research Libraries News* [cited 30 April 2000]. Available from http://www.ala.org/acrl/ resfeb99.html; INTERNET.

Greene, Howard R. 1998. *The Select: Realities of Life and Learning in America's Elite College.* New York: Cliff Street Books.

Kotlas, Carolyn. 1998. Competing with the Web: If we don't win, our users lose. *Information Outlook* 2:13–14 [cited 1 May 2000]. Available from Periodical Abstracts, <http://www.texshare.edu/ovidweb/ovidweb.cgi>.

Library of Congress. 2000. Collaborative digital reference service [cited 6 June 2000]. Available from http://www.loc.gov/rr/digiref/about.html; INTERNET.

Library of Congress. 1999. *Digital Libraries Initiative* [cited 1 May 2000]. Available from http://memory.loc.gov/ammem/dli2/; INTERNET.

Martinez, Michael J. 2000. Microsoft hires two teen consultants. *Los Angeles Times* [cited 30 April 2000]. Available from http://www.latimes.com/business/ cutting/20000427/t000039487.html; INTERNET. Link no longer valid.

Networked Digital Library of Theses and Dissertations. 2000. *Networked Digital Library of Theses and Dissertations* [cited 1 May 2000]. Available from http:// www.ndltd.org/; INTERNET.

New York University Bobst Library. 1999. *Streaming Media Services at NYU Libraries* [cited 1 May 2000]. Available from http://mediatv.bobst.nyu.edu/; INTERNET. Link no longer valid.

North Carolina State University Libraries, Digital Library Initiatives Department. 1999. *MyLibrary@NCState* [cited 1 May 2000]. Available from http:// my.lib.ncsu.edu/; INTERNET.

Odlyzko, Andrew. 1997. Silicon dreams and silicon bricks: The continuing evolution of libraries. *Library Trends* 46:152–67 [cited 1 May 2000]. Available from Periodical Abstracts, <http://www.texshare.edu/ovidweb/ovidweb.cgi>.

Olsen, Florence. 2000a. Institutions collaborate on development of free portal software. *Chronicle of Higher Education* [cited 5 May 2000]. Available from http://chronicle.com/free/2000/05/2000050501t.htm; INTERNET.

————. 2000b. U. of Pittsburgh sets pace on digital certificates. *The Chronicle of Higher Education* 46 (28 April):A47 [cited 6 June 2000]. Available from Expanded Academic ASAP, <http://infotrac.galegroup.com/>.

Pleas, Keith. 1999. Certificates, keys, and security. *PC Magazine* 19 (20 April):203 [cited 5 June 2000]. Available from Expanded Academic ASAP, <http://infotrac.galegroup.com/>.

Project Gutenberg and Promo.Net. 2000. *Project Gutenberg Official Home Site* [cited 2 May 2000]. Available from http://promo.net/pg/; INTERNET.

Raish, Martin. 2000. Academic librarians offer the crucial human element in online scholarship. *Chronicle of Higher Education* 46:B4–B5.

Rifkin, Adam. 1998. *Adam Rifkin's Generation X Page* [cited 30 April 2000]. Available from http://www.cs.caltech.edu/~adam/LEAD/genx.html; INTERNET.

Rochester Institute of Technology. 2000. *EASI: Equal Access to Software and Information* [cited 1 May 2000]. Available from http://www.rit.edu/~easi/; INTERNET.

San Diego State University. 2000. *ERes* [cited 2 May 2000]. Available from http://ecr.sdsu.edu/; INTERNET.

Tapscott, Don. 1998. *Growing Up Digital: The Rise of the Net Generation.* New York: McGraw-Hill.

University of Iowa Libraries. 2000. *Information Arcade* [cited 1 May 2000]. Available from http://www.lib.uiowa.edu/arcade/; INTERNET.

University of Southern California. 2000. *Information Commons* [cited 1 May 2000]. Available from http://www.usc.edu/isd/locations/undergrad/leavey/; INTERNET.

University of Texas System Digital Library, Digital Information Literacy Office. 2000. *TILT (Texas Information Literacy Tutorial)* [cited 1 May 2000]. Available from http://tilt.lib.utsystem.edu/; INTERNET.

University of Washington, UWired Center for Teaching, Learning & Technology. 1999. *Catalyst* [cited 1 May 2000]. Available from http://depts.washington.edu/catalyst/home.html; INTERNET.

Virginia Military Institute, Preston Library. 2000. *SourceFinder* [cited 1 May 2000]. Available from http://www.vmi.edu/sourcefinder/; INTERNET.

Virtual Reference Desk Project. 2000. *Virtual Reference Desk Project* [cited 1 May 2000]. Available from http://www.vrd.org/; INTERNET.

Wellesley College. 2000. *Knapp Media and Technology Center* [cited 1 May 2000]. Available from http://www.wellesley.edu/Knapp/center.html; INTERNET.

Widdicombe, Richard. 1994–1995. Re-engineering the college library for periodicals. *Planning for Higher Education* [cited 30 April 2000]. Available from http://www.lib.stevens-tech.edu/ill/reeng.html; INTERNET. Link no longer valid.

Yale University School of Medicine, Cushing/Whitney Medical Library. 2000. *JAKE (Jointly Administered Knowledge Environment)* [cited 1 May 2000]. Available from http://jake.med.yale.edu/; INTERNET.

Fishing for Success:
Faculty/Librarian Collaboration Nets Effective Library Assignments

Caroline Gilson and Stephanie Michel

Picture this scene: A mob of students comes to the reference desk begging for help with a library assignment that directs them to use resources the library does not own. The assignment also directs them to use resources incorrectly (such as looking in the *New York Times Index* to find an article from the day they were born) and gives no indication of where to look to find the answers to other questions on their assignment. Poorly designed library assignments frustrate librarians and aggravate students who perceive library research to be tedious, frustrating, and a waste of time. What can librarians do to stop this onslaught of bad library assignments?

At Radford University, a midsized state-supported university located in southwestern Virginia, librarians have faced the scenario described above, and many more. Motivated by the large number of misleading library assignments crossing the reference desk, the librarians at Radford University sought ways to reach out to faculty and instructors on campus to educate them about the importance of creating effective, meaningful library assignments.

Rationale: What Are We Fishing For?
Before the librarians at Radford could begin to implement strategies to improve library assignments on campus, it was necessary to explain to faculty, and to themselves, why good library assignments are important. Primarily, the librarians concluded that library assignments that have been carefully planned and researched can positively affect how students will use the library in the future. Effective library assignments can:

- *Teach students information-seeking skills:* A good library assignment can teach students the essential skills needed to conduct research and find information. These skills will apply not only to a specific assignment but also can be applied to other information-seeking experiences throughout the students' college careers.

- *Offer hands-on experience in the library*: A good library assignment can get students into the library and actually using the tools rather than just seeing them demonstrated in class. By using the tools for themselves, students are more likely to learn the necessary skills and retain what they have learned.

- *Lay a foundation for future library success:* A good library assignment will give students a positive initial experience in the library, which will affect their future perceptions and use of the library. Rather than leaving the library feeling that research is frustrating, boring, and futile, students who are given a good library assignment will feel successful in their research and be willing to use the library in the future.

Thus, a good library assignment can facilitate a student's introduction to the library and begin teaching him or her essential information-seeking skills.

Sink or Swim: Assignment Pitfalls

For the reasons described above, well-designed library assignments are an important part of the student's introduction to library research. By working with faculty to create effective library assignments, we, the librarians at Radford, hope to avoid the following scenarios:

- *The scavenger hunt*: Students are given an assignment to find specific pieces of unrelated information, that usually have no connection to course content. While doing the assignment, students run willy-nilly through the library tracking down obscure bits of trivia but ultimately leave without learning about the subject of their course or how to use the library.

- *The swarming mob scene*: Hundreds of students come to the reference desk the night before the assignment is due, asking for the same index or resource. Better yet, the library does not own the resource, or an earlier student has ripped out the page with the necessary information. Librarians are frustrated and overwhelmed, and the students perceive that library research is tiresome, difficult, and futile.

- *Go fish*: Students are given a complicated library assignment but are not given any indication of which resources might be most appropriate for their assignment. As a result, students turn to familiar resources to search for information (very likely spending hours doing futile searches on the Internet for obscure facts). Or, students might eventually ask at the reference desk, where the harried librarians can point their thirtieth customer to the appropriate resource for that question. Again, the student has learned nothing useful about library research.

- *The one that got away*: While librarians help the students in the swarming mob scene above, several students standing at the fringe of the crowd decide that it is not worth their time to wait for assistance and leave. The librarians will never know what the question was or whether they could have helped: The students are left on their own to muddle their way through the library's resources.

These are just a few examples of assignments that are disasters: They are unclear, do not teach research strategies, and drive librarians crazy because they are disorganized and unpredictable. They also illustrate what librarians do *not* want to see in the library. However, what can librarians do to improve the quality of library assignments on campus?

Top 10 Library Assignment Pitfalls

1. The mob scene: An entire class looks for one piece of information, uses one source, or researches a single topic.

2. Fill in the blanks: Students are unable to locate material because of incomplete or inaccurate references or citations.

3. Shot in the dark: Instructors assign materials that the library does not own or assume that a particular type of information is available.

4. Guessing games: Students try to locate assigned sources using citations containing nonstandard abbreviations.

5. Clue: Instructors use meaningless terms such as "semi-scholarly journals" or jargon recognizable only to scholars within the discipline.

6. Garbage in/garbage out: Instructors suggest inappropriate methods in the instructions such as "browse the journals."

7. Out of focus: Students are assigned or allowed to select research topics that are vague, far too global, or far too narrow.

8. Needle in a haystack: Students are to find the answers to obscure factual questions.

9. Scramble: Students are not given an appropriate amount of time to complete the assignment.

10.   Out in left field: Students are given an exercise that has no logical relationship to the course.

Adapted from Donegan 1989; *Designing Effective Assignments* 1999; Stevens and Engeldinger 1984; and *User Education Program Manual* 1993.

Reeling Them In: Improving Faculty Information Literacy

At Radford University, we feel it is necessary to reach out to and recruit faculty in our efforts to teach information literacy skills. In "Bridging the Great Divide: Improving Relations between Librarians and Classroom Faculty," the Wade R. Kotter states that the ultimate success of a library instruction program depends on the cooperation and partnership between faculty and librarians (1999, 299). An important first step in improving library assignments on campus is to improve the information literacy skills of the faculty. Many faculty may not be up-to-date on recent additions or changes to the library and may not be aware of the most appropriate library resources for their discipline. If the faculty are not familiar with library resources, they will be unable to guide their students through effective library research. Thus, to improve student information literacy through library assignments, it is first necessary to improve faculty information literacy.

To improve faculty information literacy, librarians must work with faculty to ensure that they are familiar with appropriate library resources for their subject area. Faculty need to know how to access those resources and how to effectively use them to find the needed information. Further, faculty need to be aware of the steps involved in ultimately accessing the information, whether it is in the library, available on a full-text resource, or attainable through interlibrary loan. After faculty are familiar with all aspects of the information-seeking process, they will be better able to encourage and assist their students in using the appropriate resources. Information-literate faculty should be able to use their skills to create better—or at least better-informed—library assignments.

Casting the Line: How You Can Reach Faculty

After a commitment is made to improve faculty information literacy skills, the difficult task of how to reach the faculty remains. They are on one side of campus, librarians are on the other, and never the twain shall meet—or so it seems. Despite the distance (physical and otherwise), there are many ways to reach out to faculty to promote information literacy and to lobby for effective library assignments. For example, librarians can:

• *Ask to be invited to a department meeting*: The advantage of a department meeting is that all the faculty in a given department can be reached at the same time. At the meeting, promote library services by encouraging faculty to bring their students to the library for instruction sessions. Or, consider offering more personalized services, such as serving as an advisor to review assignments that involve library research or assisting faculty with their personal research. Department meetings are a great opportunity for librarians to increase faculty awareness about library services and resources and for faculty to become acquainted with a librarian, whom they may feel more comfortable approaching in the future.

• *Work one-on-one with faculty and instructors*: When faculty members call to schedule a library instruction session, ask them for a description of the assignment they will be giving their students. Asking for a copy of the course syllabus can be a helpful way to get an overall feeling for the demands of that course and how library research might apply. With this information, you can tailor the instruction session to the requirements and content of the course to better serve the students' needs. It may even be possible to create, or collaborate with the faculty member to create, a library assignment for the students that reinforces the library instruction.

Furthermore, dialogue with faculty members provides an excellent opportunity to encourage their involvement in the instruction session. Jane Schillie, a librarian at Virginia Tech, once suggested a great question to pose to the faculty: What will *your* role be during the instruction session? This question can help faculty to think about their role and responsibility during the instruction and encourage them to take a more active role. Eliciting

Top 10 Ways to Create a Successful Library Assignment

1. Why are we doing this? Explain the objectives of the assignment to the students. Create a sense of its importance, emphasizing the relevance of library work to course and college education.

2. What are we supposed to do? Provide students with a written description, including what the assignment involves, what types of sources you want them to use, and the citation, call number, and location of the specific sources you expect them to use.

3. Make it relevant. Develop a library exercise that is directly applicable to course content as well as to the specific assignment.

4. Match the assignment to the skill level of students. To be safe, assume your students have minimal library knowledge.

5. Teach research strategies. Construct library instruction assignments so that students learn to develop appropriate strategies for approaching library research, including an understanding of the steps involved in the research process, discussion of different types of material, and the means of assessing it.

6. Be able to do the assignment yourself. After you have written it, try it out.

7. Make it fun. Granted, library research may not be a student's first choice of fun things to do on a Friday night, but try to make the assignment interesting. If possible, relate the assignment to the student's own interests.

8. Involve a librarian. Involve a librarian in the planning and/or presentation of the library instruction assignment. Librarians can provide useful insights into potential problem areas, as well as make suggestions about what types of sources might best suit the student's needs.

9. Leave a copy of the assignment with a librarian or at the reference desk. Knowing what to expect helps the library staff to be prepared and better able to help your students.

10. Give the assignment early. Let students know from the beginning what will be expected of them and incorporate the library assignment early enough in the semester so that the skills learned may benefit other class assignments.

Adapted from Arnsan 1993; Donegan 1989; *Designing Effective Assignments* 1999; Godin 1993; Laverty 1998; Nussbaum 1991; Stevens and Engeldinger 1984; *Tips for Effective Library Assignments* 1998; and *User Education Program Manual* 1993.

involvement from the faculty member helps to ensure success during the instruction session.

Ideally, the professor brings his classes to the library every semester for instruction. At the beginning of the session, he or she talks to the students about his or her experiences working in and using a library. Throughout the library instruction session, the professor interjects comments about the database being searched or how a particular resource will apply to the students' assignment. Because the faculty member is actively participating in the instruction session, students are more likely to be involved or ask questions. At Radford, we have found that the most successful instruction sessions are those with direct faculty involvement.

- *Reach out at campus events*: An excellent method of reaching out to a large number of faculty is to participate in campus events. Attend new faculty orientations, campus workshops, or seminars—any faculty and instructor gathering—and give a short "instruction commercial." Taking a few minutes to mention who you are and what the library can do to work with faculty will help to get the word out about library instruction.

- *Promote instruction services through campus publications*: Preexisting campus publications can be a great way to reach a large audience with a minimum of expense. Put an advertisement in the campus newspaper, write a column for the library newsletter, or publish information in other campus publications. In addition, campuswide e-mail listservs are a wonderful free resource for publicizing the library's services to a large audience.

- *Create an instruction services Web page*: As a part of the library's Web site, create a specific page with information about the library's instruction program. Outline the types of services available (such as course-related library instruction, individual research consultations, walking tours, and library workshops) and provide a list of people who can be contacted for further information, giving their names, phone numbers, and e-mail addresses.

- *Create an online tutorial to library research*: Library tutorials provide students and faculty with a valuable resource for finding information about how to use the library and conduct research. As an added advantage, Web-based tutorials are available twenty-four hours a day, at any computer (on or off campus) and can be accessed by students or faculty at their place and time of need.

Tutorials can involve a significant commitment up front, including staff time and the cost of purchasing adequate hardware and software to create and run them (such as Adobe Acrobat or screen capture software). Convincing colleagues and library administrators about the value of, and the need for, the tutorial will help to gain the support needed to complete the project and promote its use.

The strategies listed above suggest some general methods that librarians can use on almost any campus to reach out to faculty to encourage awareness and the effective use of library services and resources. The following section focuses on the techniques that have worked for the librarians at Radford University.

Luring Them In: How We Have Reached Radford University Faculty

At Radford University, we have employed several specific strategies to reach out to faculty to improve information literacy and provide forums to discuss effective library assignments. Although some of these methods are unique to our campus, many could be adapted for use at any campus.

Our Turn workshops. Our Turn is a series of campuswide workshops offered the week after graduation, before the start of summer classes. Programs are offered by faculty for faculty on a variety of topics, usually including at least one workshop offered by the library. Because of the popularity of this program, mini-Our Turn sessions are now presented in August, before the start of the fall semester, and in January, the week before the spring semester begins.

The Our Turn workshops have proved to be an effective means of reaching out to a small group of interested faculty. The library has offered workshops on topics such as the virtual library, which covered online database searching; introduction to Web searching; advanced Web searching; full-text databases; and legal and political research. The workshops help faculty to improve their information literacy skills, and provide us with an opportunity to advertise the library's services.

Our Turn has also provided us with an excellent opportunity to converse with faculty about library assignments. One of the library's Our Turn workshops devoted a whole afternoon to the topic "Creating Effective Library Assignments." During this session, we emphasized that faculty must think carefully before giving library assignments, taking into consideration what the students may already know or not know and what skills they need to do the assignment. The workshop addressed the importance of outlining clear objectives and expectations for the library assignment and the importance of relating the assignment to the content of the course. It also focused on library assignment Do's and Don'ts and suggested creative alternatives to the "traditional" library assignment. The handouts and content prepared for that session later evolved into the library newsletter insert and handout titled, "Library Assignments: The Good, the Bad, and the FISHY!

During Our Turn, the university caters lunches that are attended by most of the faculty. At one of these lunches, we took the initiative to do a brief commercial for library instruction, which allowed us to reach a large number of people at one time. Overall, Our Turn has provided the library with an ideal forum to work with faculty and increase knowledge and awareness of the library on campus.

Electronic information workshops. Each semester, McConnell Library offers workshops that are open to all students, faculty, and staff. The

---

Creative Library Assignments

Try these as creative alternatives to a traditional library assignment:

- Ask students to prepare an annotated bibliography on a topic of their choice.

- Ask students to prepare an abstract of a journal article.

- Ask students to find and compare a popular magazine article and a scholarly article on the same topic.

- Ask students to research the issues and participate in a panel discussion or debate.

- Ask students to find and compare book reviews on a book relevant to the subject of the course. (Hint: provide students with a list of appropriate books.)

Credits: Designing Effective Assignments 1999; Tips for Effective Library Assignments 1998

---

workshops provide an opportunity to promote library services and to improve information literacy skills. We ask participants to register (preferably at least a day in advance) and limit participation to twenty people. Over time, the workshops have evolved. Originally, we offered workshops on a single resource or database at varying times throughout the morning and afternoon. Later, we experimented with moving the workshops to the evening—from 6:00 P.M. to 6:45 P.M. In our experience, evening workshops have attracted the most participants, so we have continued to offer them at this time. In addition, we converted the workshops from database specific to subject focused: that is, instead of teaching a workshop on PsycINFO, we offered one on Resources for Psychology, where we could talk about one or two resources central to psychology research. These changes have resulted in higher student and faculty participation.

Attendance at the workshops has reached the twenty-person maximum only once, when extra credit was offered for attending the session. In general, attendance has averaged three to five people per session. Although we wish the sessions were better attended, those students and faculty who do attend leave with a greater understanding of library services and improved information literacy skills.

Department meetings. Another effective means of reaching out to faculty is to participate in department meetings. However, as a twist, instead of asking to be invited to meetings in each department's building, we invited faculty to schedule one of their department meetings in the McConnell Library classroom. During each of those meetings, an instruction librarian utilized our electronic classroom to demonstrate resources

Fishy Library Assignment Scenario:

Can you relate to the following situation?

A group of students approach the reference desk, asking where the encyclopedias are located. The reference librarian points them in the right direction, later noticing the students becoming more frustrated and anxious as they look up information. The reference librarian approaches the group and asks if they are finding what they need. One of the bewildered students hands their assignment to the librarian: *Find the following fifty terms, define, and explain their importance to Western Civilization.* "Our history professor said the answers could be found at the library," another student said.

BAD elements:

• No bibliography of sources for students to consult

• Little or no focus or tie-in to class

• Students assume an encyclopedia is the best source to use

The IMPROVED Library Assignment Scenario: What a Catch!

A group of students comes into the library and heads to the reference section. A history professor has given out lists of five terms covering specific time periods and events in history. Each student has a bibliography of sources to examine, which was prepared by a reference librarian. Prior to the assignment, a librarian met with the class and discussed the resources available for doing research for this class. For this assignment, students are to look up each assigned term in two sources, compare the information presented, and write a paragraph per assigned term on their findings. Though the assignment takes time, the students are challenged and realize the importance and variety of information resources.

GOOD elements:

• Includes a bibliography of sources to consult

• Assignment structure is manageable, more focused

• Reference librarian participation introduced resources, provided an accurate source list, and saved long-term research headaches!

relevant to the department's discipline. This also proved to be a good time to talk about the availability of instruction sessions for their courses and to review collection development information. Several departments responded to our initial invitation, and others expressed interest in attending sometime in the future. Through these department meetings, we were able to educate all faculty in a department at one time about library resources and services.

One-on-one consultation. To increase our accessibility, we have made ourselves available to faculty for individual consultation. We serve as research mentors, encouraging faculty to schedule appointments with us to get advice and assistance on how to proceed with their research projects. In addition, we consult with faculty on library assignments. We encourage faculty to send us a copy of their library assignment, which allows instruction librarians to examine the assignment and make suggestions about resources or pathways that may have changed since the faculty created the assignment and also gives reference librarians the opportunity to determine which resources would be most appropriate and lets them know what to expect. Ultimately, this collaboration has helped to remove common errors from library assignments and has resulted in effective library assignments that more accurately introduce the library's resources.

In our one-on-one conversations with faculty, we sometimes have the opportunity to create a library assignment for a class. For instance, Stephanie Michel collaborated with an instructor to create an exercise on our online tutorial, the Highlander Guide. The assignment was distributed and completed during the instruction session. Stephanie subsequently graded the assignments and returned them to the instructor to be included in the students' grades. This proved to be a useful method of reinforcing the students' learning by requiring them to complete a well-designed library assignment. This arrangement also allowed Stephanie to see what the students had learned.

Through these one-on-one dialogues with faculty, a relationship is established with faculty members and librarians gain a better understanding of their courses. As a result, librarians are in a better position to work directly with faculty toward the goal of improving library assignments.

Faculty attendance at instruction sessions. Another method of teaching faculty information literacy skills is through the instruction sessions they schedule for their students. If faculty who are faithful about bringing their classes to the library are encouraged to attend, listen, and participate in the instruction session, they will learn or reinforce their knowledge of the resources being taught. Many times, after teaching a course-related instruction session, we have been approached by the faculty member who confided that he or she also learned something new. As an added benefit, when students see the faculty member involved in the instruction session, especially if the faculty member emphasizes the importance of library research to the class, they are more likely to see the importance of library research and pay attention. Steve McKinzie of Dickinson College observed that "Faculty comments...can increase (an instruction) session's effectiveness remarkably" (1997, 20). Thus, while providing the opportunity to expand their students' library and information literacy skills, faculty can make valuable contributions and also may benefit themselves from the instruction session.

Highlander Guide. Finally, we have used, the Highlander Guide (http://lib.runet.edu/hguide) as a means of improving faculty information literacy. We publicize it in instruction sessions, on the library's Web site, in Our Turn workshops (we also offer an entire workshop on the Highlander Guide), and in department meetings as a means of learning about how to use the library. Our online tutorial is always available at any time of day or night to any student or faculty member who is interested in learning more about library services or how to conduct library research. As an added bonus, faculty do not have to admit that they need help to benefit from this resource.

After They Are Hooked: Some Final Thoughts

After the process of communicating with faculty about information literacy and library assignments is initiated, there are a few things to keep in mind:

- **Keep a sense of HUMOR!** As with everything in the library, it helps to be able to see the humor in any situation. The ability to roll with the punches and keep a brave face when the computers crash in the middle of an instruction session helps to keep things in perspective. Someday you *will* be able to look back on today's disaster and laugh.

- **Offer praise and encouragement.** A little praise can go a long way. Praise faculty for bringing their classes to the library and for their willingness to work with you on their library assignments. Faculty who have been "converted" to library instruction can be great assets for spreading the word within their departments. Praise may help to reinforce the importance of the library's role in their class and may keep faculty coming back for more.

  Praise and encouragement do not have to be limited to faculty. Praise and encourage each other within the library. Share your success stories with one other to help spread the word about what works. Also, be there to encourage and support each other when everything does not go as planned and look for ways to improve. The shared encouragement and collaboration will see you through the rough times and boost your confidence when things go well.

- **Evaluate the instruction program.** Evaluating your instruction program can provide some invaluable feedback about others' perceptions of your services and can help you to determine the program's overall success. Evaluations can also provide valuable suggestions for improving library instruction. They can take many forms: pre- and posttests during an instruction session, evaluation forms given upon completion of a research assignment, or forms distributed to selected classes at the end of the semester. Questions might include: What was the most and least helpful aspect of the instruction session? Did the library instruction session provide useful information that will assist you with your research? What was your overall reaction to the instruction session?

At McConnell Library, we are just beginning to formally evaluate our instruction program. Upon completion of the Our Turn workshops and Electronic Information workshops, we usually distribute a brief evaluation form to collect student feedback and to elicit suggestions for future topics. This feedback has helped us to shape future programs.

In the spring of 1999, we surveyed the students of freshman writing courses who had been exposed to the Highlander Guide. The survey was designed to elicit the students' perceptions and use of the tutorial. Overall, students and faculty reported very favorable reactions to the Highlander Guide. The most positive reviews came from a select group of students who had been required to use the Highlander Guide as a class assignment. Moreover, students who were already comfortable with using the Web or the library to locate information reported more positive remarks overall. However, the most surprising result of the survey was the discovery that students, and especially faculty, preferred traditional library instruction over the exclusive use of the online tutorial. The results provided many interesting insights into the use and perceptions of the Highlander Guide.

In the spring of 2000, we distributed surveys in selected course-related instruction sessions to gather immediate feedback about the instruction session. The one-page survey included questions about the instruction presentation and asked students to report how useful they believed it would be to their research. Students were also asked to comment on the overall instruction session.

Preliminary results from the 448 surveys gathered showed that the majority of students expressed positive views about the instruction sessions. Ninety-seven percent of the students surveyed thought that the session provided useful information that would assist with research for that class. Over 89 percent expressed confidence in their ability to use the resources presented during the instruction session.

At the end of the semester, a second one-page survey was sent to the same classes. This survey asked students to reflect on the instruction session and answer questions based on what they had learned and how the session had helped with their research. Of the 294 responses, 84 percent of the respondents reported that the instruction session provided useful information for their research and 86 percent felt confident in using the resources presented during the instruction session.

Our initial analysis of the data showed that students' confidence levels and perceptions of the usefulness of the instruction remained high, both immediately after library instruction and later in the semester. However, in both cases, the percentages dropped slightly in the follow-up survey.

It is possible that when the resources were demonstrated during the instruction session, students felt confident that they would be able to use them on their own. However, when the students attempted to independently conduct their research, they may have forgotten how to use the resources or discovered that research was not as easy as they had initially perceived. It is also possible that this decrease may be explained by other factors, such as technical glitches, poorly defined topics, or student procrastination, which may have made it difficult to access or find information. We anticipate conducting further analysis and a review of the literature to aid us in drawing further conclusions from these data.

Through humor and praise, you can sustain yourself and others and help to maintain your sanity through a hectic instruction session. Through evaluation, you can look back on what you have done well and look ahead to what can be improved in the future.

The "Hook": Our Instruction Ideology

Give a man a fish; you have fed him for today. Teach a man to fish; and you have fed him for a lifetime.

—Author unknown

This quote sums up the philosophy of library instruction at Radford University: rather than doing the research for them, librarians must attempt to teach students (and faculty) how to independently find the information they need and achieve self-sufficiency in today's information world. Marion C. Winner of Northern Kentucky University encourages librarians to be "proactive" and "fully prepared…in teaching students how to utilize technology to access information" (1998, 26). By reaching out to faculty and improving their information literacy skills, librarians enhance their knowledge of the library and facilitate their creation of effective library assignments. Ultimately, these library assignments will guide students through the development of their own information literacy skills, which will assist them in future information-seeking endeavors throughout their college career and will help to promote and encourage lifelong learning.

References

Arnsan, Daniel C. 1993. Resources, research, results: Librarian and instructor, partners in student success. *Innovation Abstracts* 15(3). ERIC, ED 405906.

Designing effective assignments: Library assignment tips. 1999. Austin, Tex.: University of Texas at Austin, UT Library Online [cited 19 March 1999]. Available from http://www.lib.utexas.edu/Libs/UGL/DILO/ dilo_assignments1.htm; INTERNET. Link no longer valid.

Donegan, Patricia Morris. 1989. Creating effective library assignments: A workshop for faculty. Paper presented at a poster session at the Annual Conference of the American Library Association, Dallas, Tex., 26 June. ERIC, ED 329260.

Godin, Christine C. 1993. Buried treasure. *Innovation Abstracts* 15(18). ERIC, ED 405906.

Kotter, Wade R. 1999. Bridging the great divide: Improving relations between librarians and classroom faculty. *Journal of Academic Librarianship* 25(4):294–303.

Laverty, Cory. 1998. Designing library assignments. Kingston, Ontario, Canada: Queen's University, Queen's University Libraries [cited 26 March 1999]. Available from http://stauffer.queensu.ca/inforef/instruct/design.htm; INTERNET.

McKinzie, Steve. 1997. Librarians and faculty in tandem: Taking our cue from the evening news. *Reference & User Services Quarterly* 37(1):19–21.

Nussbaum, Francis E. 1991. Introduce successful library assignments to students in biological sciences. *American Biology Teacher* 53(5):301–4.

Schillie, Jane. 1998. Conversation with the authors, 2 April.

Stevens, Barbara R., and Eugene A. Engeldinger. 1984. Library instruction within the curriculum: The sciences, business and nursing. Projects developed for a faculty development seminar. Eau Claire, Wisc.: University of Wisconsin. ERIC, ED 266789.

Tips for effective library assignments. 1998. Greensboro, N.C.: University of North Carolina at Greensboro, Walter Clinton Jackson Library [cited 2 April 1999]. Available from http://library.uncg.edu/depts/ref/refinstruction/libtips.html; INTERNET. Link no longer valid.

User education program manual. 1993. Santa Barbara: University of California. ERIC, ED 366082.

Winner, Marion C. 1998. Librarians as partners in the classroom: An increasing imperative. *Reference Services Review* 26(1):25–30.

The Greatest Problem with Which the Library Is Confronted:
A Survey of Academic Library Outreach to the Freshman Course

Cindy Pierard and Kathryn Graves

Introduction

The Freshman Year Experience movement has created an excellent opportunity for academic library outreach. Its values, which include collaboration among various campus units charged with supporting student success and a focus on student mastery of key academic skills, correspond well with the objective of many college and university libraries: to become a more central part of the institution's educational mission. This chapter provides a discussion of academic library outreach to one of the movement's most significant components, the freshman course. The aim is to provide an overview of both the historical development of and contemporary trends in postsecondary freshman programming and corresponding library outreach efforts. A final section explores research findings related to student outcomes.

Origins and Evolution of the Freshman Course Concept

> It is generally recognized that the most pressing problem of higher education in America today is the care of the underclassman, the Freshman, and the sophomores…[this care] naturally divides itself into two elements, training in personal habits and training in scholarship….Whatever the system of handling Freshmen, there should be an evident purpose behind it, and this purpose should be a moral one (Jordan 1910, 442).

What are the problems associated with retaining today's college freshmen? The 1999–2000 report of the Consortium for Student Retention Data Exchange (CSRDE) reported that more than half of the students who leave an institution do so during their freshman year. The picture is especially grim for minority students, with some studies finding the departure rate for black and Hispanic students to be approximately twice the rate for white students (Tinto 1993; CSRDE 2000).

The authors would like to extend their appreciation to Kathryn Nemeth Tuttle, director, Freshman-Sophomore Advising Center at the University of Kansas, who graciously shared her knowledge of the history of American higher education and whose input strengthened several sections of this chapter.

Because the first year of college is a particularly critical time for attrition, colleges and universities have implemented a variety of programs designed to help new students with this transition. Included among those programs are the development of incentives for faculty who work with freshmen, an enhanced and expanded model of precollege orientation, reinforcement of tutoring and study skills workshops, programs that address the role of student advising, and programs designed for specific freshman populations such as minority, commuter, international, and nontraditional students. One of the most persistent programmatic responses has been the development of a special class designed specifically for freshmen, often called the freshman seminar or freshman orientation course (Gardner, Decker, and McNairy 1986).

Although the vast majority of freshman orientation courses were developed after 1980, it should be noted that various forms of "the freshman course" have long been a part of American higher education. One of the first formal orientation programs was offered by Boston University more than one hundred years ago (1888) with emphases on helping students adapt to the physical environment, social structure, and academic requirements and expectations of the institution. In 1900, Oberlin College initiated the first required noncredit freshman orientation course in the country, and in 1911, Reed College offered the first for-credit course, which covered topics such as the purpose of the college, student honesty, intercollegiate athletics, and college religion (Gordon 1989).

Growth in freshman programming spread rapidly in the first two decades of the twentieth century and particularly in the years following World War I as a reaction to the steady democratization of universities and the rise of the student personnel movement. Students from diverse social and academic backgrounds were arriving on college campuses with different goals for their education, including social and vocational goals that they held to be as important as, if not more important than, traditional intellectual values. American universities began to seek some means of addressing the difference between the more traditional German model of the research university, with its emphasis on intellectual rigor and specialized graduate study, and the aspirations—many of them decidedly nonintellectual—of this new, more diverse student body. One significant response was to develop an array of student personnel services covering functions such as athletics, discipline, educational testing, financial aid, mental and physical health, and vocational guidance. The aim was to better integrate the curricular and extracurricular aspects of student life and to help ensure that both the intellectual and nonintellectual needs of students were met. A direct outcome of this concern with developing "the whole student" was considerable expansion of the freshman course concept:

> For general guidance, the device most often resorted to was some
> form of orientation course or program. In a number of cases, this

assumed the definite form of a "Freshman Week," an introductory period of from one to seven days preceding the regular work of the term and devoted to the task of adjusting the entering student to his new environment. In contrast to this, the general orientation course, while attacking much the same problem, extended the time over a longer period varying from two weeks to a full college year.... Courses of this type usually tried to teach freshmen how to use the library, how to study, what the purposes and aims of the college were, and how to participate in campus activities (Brubacher and Rudy 1997, 343).

In 1916, only six colleges had implemented for-credit orientation courses. A decade later, in 1926, this number jumped to eighty-two schools, including Princeton, Columbia, Pittsburgh, Syracuse, Johns Hopkins, Indiana, Missouri, and Stanford (Gordon 1989). A review of the literature of this period reflects the growth of the freshman orientation movement. In the bibliography for their comprehensive monograph, *The Construction of Orientation Courses for College Freshmen*, Fitts and Swift (1928) referenced 116 articles published between 1910 and 1927 concerning the unique needs of college freshmen and the development of effective orientation programs.

In the ensuing five decades, a variety of societal forces influenced higher education, shifting the emphasis on the importance of freshman orientation. For example, the enrollment boom following World War II (encouraged by the G.I. Bill of 1944) and later expansions in the 1970s promoted an increase in orientation efforts as university administrators struggled to provide adequate housing and to address the concerns of a more heterogeneous student body. Other periods such as the Great Depression and the Vietnam era stifled efforts as administrative personnel found themselves either financially exhausted or distracted by greater forces of social upheaval (Levine 1978).

The steady growth and diversification of the student body has been an undeniable force in the development of twentieth-century American higher education. In his recent study of college students, Arthur Levine noted that "between 1900, when 4 percent of all eighteen-year-olds attended college, and 1997, when 65 percent of all high school graduates continued to some form of post-secondary education, the nation moved from what has been characterized as elite to mass to universal higher education" (Levine 1998, 145). This dramatic shift has presented considerable challenges to colleges and universities. Some critics have charged that the response has been slow and uneven.

In 1993, the Wingspread Group, a foundation-sponsored assembly of some sixteen prominent educators and policymakers, issued a damning report entitled *An American Imperative: Higher Expectations for Higher Education*. The report was sharply critical of the state of American higher education, finding that colleges and universities handed out credentials rather than focusing on actual student learning and that the pursuit of research money had led many institutions too far from an emphasis on excellence in teaching. Colleges and universities were doing a poor job of articulating their expectations and preparing students to meet high standards: "Like the rest of American education, the nation's colleges and universities appear to live by an unconscious educational rule of thumb that their function is to weed out, not to cultivate, students for whom they have accepted responsibility" (Wingspread Group 1993, 1).

These calls for accountability, coupled with a need for increased tuition dollars, caused many postsecondary institutions to take a hard look at both the broader research on student persistence and more specific studies of successful institutional responses to attrition. Since the mid-1970s, Vincent Tinto and others have extensively researched student persistence in various types of academic institutions. Tinto's model of student retention focuses on the integration of the individual student within his or her institutional environment, both socially and academically. Higher persistence rates are related to positive involvement with faculty and students, outside the classroom as well as within. Involvement is particularly essential during the freshman year when attrition rates are high because of factors such as lack of academic preparation, perceived lack of curricular relevance, financial pressures, transitional difficulties that may result in feelings of social isolation, and uncertainty about academic and career goals.

Tinto's research has encouraged colleges and universities to develop programs such as freshman seminars, mentoring partnerships, and shared learning communities. It has also resulted in numerous studies undertaken by other researchers (e.g., Braxton, Sullivan, and Johnson 1997; Braxton, Vesper, and Hossler 1995; Levitz, Noel, and Richter 1999; Pascarella and Terenzini 1983; Stage 1989) whose work supports and reinforces Tinto's basic tenet: the greater the students' integration into the campus environment, the greater the chance that they will persist until graduation. Considering the amount of academic attention and research devoted to student persistence, it is perhaps not surprising that approximately 70 percent of American colleges and universities recently reported that they have developed some type of freshman seminar or first-year course. Although these may vary in design and scope, the overwhelming majority of them (about 70%) "are designed to provide students with essential strategies and information to enhance the likelihood of their retention and academic/social success" (National Resource Center 2000). Some features of these courses and other current trends in programming for first-year students are discussed in a later section of this chapter.

"Strange Books, Strange People, Strange Tools": The Origins of Library Outreach to Freshman Seminar Programs

> It is my belief that every college should offer and require some kind of training in the use of the library. I also believe that this

> training should begin with the freshman year.... I have found that
> the freshmen provide the greatest problem with which the library
> is confronted (English 1926, 779).

Many of the early freshman programs described in the previous section included the use of the library as a key skill to be taught. For example, one of the five aims of Amherst's President Alexander Meiklejohn in his conceived orientation course in 1914 was "to teach Freshmen to use the library, read newspapers and magazines, make reports and carry on discussions of live topics and issues.... Teach them to think, if possible" (Fitts and Swift 1928, 159). Soon thereafter, Brown University introduced a required freshman course of Orientation Lectures, in which one of the objectives was "to describe the libraries, laboratories, and the other facilities for study" (160).

Despite the inclusion of library skills as a key objective, the execution of actual library instruction for first-year courses was rather uneven. In their 1928 study concerning the development of freshman orientation courses, Fitts and Swift found that only ten of the forty-two institutions surveyed (23.8%) offered a library instruction component in their orientation courses. In comparison, 71.4 percent included how-to-study methods, 40.5 percent presented information on college life and activities, and 26.2 percent addressed vocational guidance.

Before World War I, most orientation courses focused on morality, college life in general, and information on the specific academic institution. Much of the early library work with freshmen was directed toward simple orientation: "An acquaintance with the library at the start should overcome the initial lack of assurance and the frightened and scared hesitancy about unfamiliar things—strange rooms, strange books, strange people, strange tools" (Drury 1928, 1024).

In the mid- to late 1920s, librarians indicated growing concern at students' apparent lack of library skills and librarians' ability to effectively teach all that was needed. In 1926, Ada Jeanette English, librarian at the New Jersey College for Women, decided "to find out, if possible, how other college librarians felt about the freshman problem and what was being done toward training students in the logical use of the library" (780). Her question apparently resonated with many librarians: She enjoyed an 88 percent response rate to the 116 questionnaires she sent to colleagues. Although the majority (57%) did not find freshmen to be more of a problem than any other students, those who did cited student unfamiliarity with libraries as the foremost problem. Respondents went on to note that they did not feel that their incoming students received adequate preparation in library skills at the secondary level, and many contended that the only way to resolve the situation was to institute a course on library skills: "A library course in the college curriculum ... develops better research students and sends out graduates equipped with familiarity in the use of books and libraries, who for this reason will be more valuable as teachers or workers in any field" (782). Deterrents to providing the necessary level of instruction will resonate with many contemporary readers: too few staff to develop and teach the courses, too little space, and insufficient funding from university administrators.

The problems voiced by English's survey respondents resurfaced throughout the next few decades and included despair over how to teach library skills effectively in a single hour (Eldridge 1928) and concern for how best to work with students who found library instruction irrelevant and unnecessary (Young 1937). Librarians often found the instruction window provided to them by traditional freshman seminar courses to be inadequate and ill timed: "students are still too preoccupied with becoming acquainted with their instructors and textbooks and making general adjustments to college life" (Hartz 1964, 78). In many cases, librarians argued that no real introduction of skills could be approached until students arrived at a more teachable moment when the skills were actually called for by an assignment, such as in introductory composition courses.

Librarians developed various responses to these challenges. Whereas some continued to provide a brief library orientation tour and/or lecture during Freshman Orientation Week or within the context of a general freshman orientation course, others decided to focus their first-year outreach efforts on introductory subject courses such as composition or English I. Yet another development in the early to mid-twentieth century was the establishment of credit and noncredit courses on library skills. Then, as now, there was ongoing debate on whether library instruction courses should be credit or noncredit and required or elective: "If it is required of all freshmen, there is likely to be much disturbance in the reading rooms, and if not required, it is often not elected by the students who need it most" (Little 1936, 19).

One trend surfacing in the 1930s was the move to assess student library skills more formally and to redirect instruction to meet those needs. Margaret Barkley, librarian at Towson State Teachers College (Maryland), administered a four-part preliminary test to incoming freshmen that measured their knowledge in the general use of books and libraries, locating information, arranging lists, and identifying sources (1939). Upon reviewing the test results, she would provide "directional arrows" to freshmen to help acclimate them to library services and resources. Similarly, librarians at the Teachers College of Kansas City began their nine-session orientation with a test of basic library skills. Accompanying the text, *The Library Key,* was "instruction in classification, shelf arrangement, parts of a book, alphabetizing, the catalogue, reference books, magazine indexes, abbreviations, and bibliography, followed by a final skills assessment" (Meyering and Pierson 1939, 448). The tests offered "a convenient, effective method of determining in which areas a class needs specific instruction, indicating what the results of definite training are, and most important of all, introducing the individual to the resources of his library" (449).

In addition to conducting formal skills assessments, librarians continued to demonstrate an interest in developing other forms of evaluation for their outreach efforts: "although wisely-planned instruction in the use of books and the library might be very useful and stimulating to a great many students, a poorly advised program might have the unfortunate result of not only discouraging but also irritating and repulsing the ordinary student who might otherwise have drifted into a passable use of the library if he had not been forcefully subjected to an unjustifiable annoyance" (James 1941, 404).

The enrollment boom following World War II challenged librarians, in part because of difficulties in working with larger classes, but also because of a lack of agreement as to what instruction should be provided or whether instruction was even useful. Despite these broader trends, the literature attests to a variety of freshman library programs (Erickson 1949; Merritt 1956; Marteena 1956). The 1960s saw a renewed interest in instruction, with librarians reaching out to teaching faculty and seeking to develop partnerships for improved library instruction programs that moved beyond the freshman tour and extended through the junior and senior years (Hartz 1964). Of particular interest to librarians in the 1950s and onward was the use of technologies such as transparencies, slides and films, closed-circuit television, and computer-assisted instruction as a means of working with larger classes (McCoy 1962; Salony 1995).

During the period of educational reform in the 1970s, librarians gained a stronger foothold as educators in the use of the library and its resources, which has carried through to the present. Although academic librarians had historically played a limited role in orientation and instruction for students, members of the profession now advocated a stronger educational role, moving them beyond being "keepers of the books" to actively demonstrating how those books (and other tools such as catalogs, indexes, and bibliographies) could be used in support of classroom instruction.

Other, more recent developments within the field of library instruction include a shift away from the teaching of particular resources to concept-based instruction. Many librarians have embraced these pedagogical shifts and have altered their approach to all levels of instruction accordingly. Thus, even the one-shot programs that continue to dominate library instruction at the postsecondary level have been infused with an emphasis on teaching concepts as well as specific resources, incorporating active learning techniques and using individual instruction sessions as foundations for the greater goal of fostering lifelong learning among students. More direct evidence of this emphasis may be found in the section discussing current trends in library outreach to freshman programs.

Of FIGS and Forums: Trends in Programming for First-year Students

Contemporary freshman courses may be divided into three general areas: those that are primarily orientation based; those that have a stronger academic focus or content; and those that attempt a mixture of both. Although content areas may overlap, orientation courses tend to focus on basic adjustment and academic skills such as learning about student government or developing test-taking skills. In contrast, seminar-type courses tend to be topically driven, with a greater emphasis on intellectual rigor (Gordon 1989). However, a growing number of first-year courses attempt to cover both areas and the terms "freshman seminar" or "freshman orientation" are often used interchangeably. Courses may be elective or required and may carry different credits. Some are offered prior to the beginning of the first year as "bridge" programs that provide earlier opportunities for adjustment. In addition to formal classes, many colleges and universities have developed extracurricular programs such as living–learning halls or peer mentoring programs in an effort to help first-year students develop learning communities that foster both social and academic development.

Orientation courses are found at a large variety of two-year and four-year colleges and universities. Examples include the Freshman Year Experience: Learning Strategies for College Students at the University of Missouri; CAS 002 at the University of Pittsburgh; University 100 at California State University, Long Beach; College 101 at Southampton College; UNV 101 at Northern Kentucky University; GENS 101V—Freshman Seminar at Montana State University; and the Becoming a Master Student program, which is widely taught at community colleges and four-year state colleges. As mentioned above, these classes focus on building social and academic skills such as library use, test-taking, time management, health awareness, career planning, and academic advising. They tend to be discussion oriented and may be taught by graduate students, academic advisors, student affairs personnel, or faculty.

Freshman seminars or symposia are offered at many liberal arts colleges such as Amherst College, Carleton College, Earlham College, Lawrence University, Southwestern University, and Williams College, and models are also in place at Harvard University and the University of California at Berkeley. These seminars are often based on a broad theme, such as American Culture: Tradition and Trends (Southwestern) and Evolution and Intellectual Revolution (Amherst), or they propose a general cross-disciplinary study of canonical and counter-canonical thought as with Freshman Studies I-II (Lawrence). Freshman seminar courses frequently include explorations of the idea of the modern university/college and core liberal arts values such as critical inquiry, careful reading, and writing. The cultivation of close working relationships between students and faculty members is also a strong theme. For example, Harvard University's Freshman Seminar brings together members of the faculty to work in partnership with first-year students to explore mutual research interests in such diverse courses as Dress and Identity in Britain, France, and the United States: 1750–1930; The Workplace: The Roles of Business, Labor, and Government; and The Hindu Temple.

Perhaps one of the clearest examples of a "blended" freshman course is the University 101 program at the University of South Carolina (USC). The course was initiated as a response to both the student riots of the 1960s and the accompanying period of declining enrollments and reduced budgets. It was designed to focus on the needs of individual students, particularly previously neglected groups, such as first-generation, adult, and minority students, to help them succeed in adjusting academically and socially to college life. In 1986, USC expanded its research base by establishing the National Resource Center for the First-Year Experience and Students in Transition. The center, which both draws from and serves as a research arm for University 101, has positioned itself as the nation's foremost resource on freshman retention.

University 101 is an elective course available to all freshmen and first-year transfer students for three credits and a letter grade. Some colleges such as Engineering and Business Administration require the course; probationary students must also take University 101. In the 1997–1998 school year, faculty taught 116 sections, which enrolled approximately 80 percent of the freshmen. In addition to regular "skills" sections, the course also includes intensive reading and writing components. A newer development is to link University 101 student sections to students pursuing a particular major or academic interest as a means of strengthening peer support and/or providing a more focused point of application for the more general study skills components. These special sections have included students in the academic programs of business, education, and history and have also targeted evening students, honors students, and international students. This "linking" component is beginning to show up in other traditional orientation courses as well (George Mason University, University of Hawaii). Finally, it is noteworthy that the goals of University 101, and the goals of an increasing number of those programs modeled on it, are directed not only at entering students but also at faculty development. Thus, these programs include mandatory training and support for all faculty and instructional staff participants.

In addition to the freshman course, a number of innovations in programming have attempted to build on and enrich the classroom experience. One of the more recent developments is the emergence of freshman interest groups (FIGs). The common goal of FIG programs is to encourage the development of student learning communities. This goal is generally achieved by co-enrolling students in common classes such as core English or math classes or introductions to a particular discipline, or by requiring some other type of common group experience through either a special group academic seminar or common residence hall assignment (Tinto and Goodsell 1993; Student success story 1996). FIG programs have been implemented at a wide range of institutions, from large state universities such as the Universities of Oregon, Washington, Wyoming, Montana, and Missouri to smaller two- and four-year colleges such as Seattle Central and LaGuardia Community Colleges.

Increasingly, programs for first-year students are taking advantage of new technologies. A particularly strong example is found in the University of Washington's UWired program, which is described as "a model project for integrating electronic communication and information navigation skills into instruction and learning on campus" (University of Washington n.d.). The UWired program, which began in 1984, has included various methods of incorporating technology and teaching, including sponsorship of a year-long technology seminar for first-year students, loans of laptop computers to participating students, and intensive instruction in library and comput-ing skills with direct academic application. UWired has evolved to work with numerous special groups on campus such as FIGs, student athletes, the campus writing program, and even state and regional groups.

Other innovative programs target specific subgroups of first-year stu-dents such as honors students, adult students, minorities, commuters, stu-dents with disabilities, and students identified as being academically at-risk. Fordham University's Excel program offers special sections of its under-graduate core curriculum classes to new and continuing adult students. The sections focus on those teaching methods that are designed to facilitate adult student learning—such as the incorporation of life experience—and most classes are offered in the evenings. Other programs for adult students em-phasize flexible scheduling, weekend seminars or other programs that pro-mote student interaction, and targeted orientation sessions (Tinto 1993). The Running Start program at Northern Kentucky University (NKU) is designed for students with basic skill deficiencies. The summer bridge pro-gram consists of a six-credit-hour package focusing on writing or math skills and a general studies class, SOC 100, all of which are supplemented by tutoring support. Students in Running Start are co-enrolled in sections of NKU's freshman orientation course, UNV 100, in the fall. The STEP pro-gram at Vincennes University provides course instruction, advising, mentoring, tutoring, and monitored study for cohort groups of students with learning disabilities. The Mississippi Alliance for Minority Participa-tion works to increase the number of minority students who enter one of the state's eight public universities in math, science, or engineering. The program begins with a summer bridge component that gives incoming stu-dents an opportunity to take an elective and a lab course related to their interest and to meet other students before the start of the academic year. In the fall, students are assigned a peer mentor (generally, a junior or a senior) and a study group. They also have the chance to get hands-on experience by assisting in a faculty research project. Alliance programs may be found in other regions, such as the Southern Rocky Mountain or Buffalo Area SUNY · Region Alliance, and at individual institutions such as the University of Virginia, the University of Texas, and Georgia Tech.

Regardless of the institutional type or the specific group of students being targeted, successful programs for first-year students tend to share certain features: the clear introduction of institutional expectations and subsequent programs that emphasize sources of support to meet those expectations; a genuine concern for not only retaining but also educating students; and a good understanding of the complex interplay of social and academic factors in student development (Tinto 1993).

Current Patterns in Academic Library Involvement with Freshman Courses

Although libraries have long been a part of freshman orientation programs, there have been increased opportunities for outreach as the freshman-year experience movement has matured during the past decade. The strengthening and expansion of library instruction within the field of librarianship has also had a significant impact on how librarians approach orientation and instruction for first-year students.

In terms of both orientation courses and academic seminars, the typical pattern of library involvement takes two general forms that have not changed markedly over time: the provision of a library orientation tour or other general instruction session(s), and the administration of some type of exercise, assignment, or research paper designed to make use of library resources.

USCs University 101 mandates a general library orientation tour, as well as several informational chapters and a follow-up exercise on the library in the course textbook, *Transitions*. The focus extends beyond mastering the use of core library resources into evaluating how well the information found benefits the student's paper or class presentation (Gardner, Decker, and McNairy 1986). University 101 is also somewhat unique in that all faculty who teach the course take part in a mandatory four-day instructor training program, which stresses innovative teaching techniques, an orientation to the academic and social needs of first-year students, and sessions with instructional support staff from the library as well as other campus units. Faculty are encouraged to supplement the basic library orientation program by adding library research components to other writing or research tasks they develop for their students.

There are several other variations on the form of library outreach to freshman orientation courses. The library components for the University of Kansas's PRE101—Orientation Seminar require that students first complete an online tutorial, which introduces library services and resources and reinforces key concepts through an interactive quiz. Students then come to the library for hands-on sessions involving key electronic resources such as the online catalog and several periodical databases. Both the tutorial and an assignment that accompanies the hands-on session are graded, and students' scores are factored into their overall course grade. Questions about the library are also incorporated into midterm and final exams. The month-long Freshman Summer Institute incorporates additional library components: In addition to the orientation provided through PRE101, students enroll in one of several elective courses (introductions to anthropology, history, English composition, environmental studies, etc.), which typically include a course-related research project for which library staff provide instruction.

In their 1995 article, Ury and King reported that library staff at Northwest Missouri State University (NMSU) provide a self-paced online library guide/follow-up quiz and a library treasure hunt to new freshmen. In addition, library staff members train student peer advisors to conduct walking tours during the orientation week prior to the fall semester. All components are designed with an informational focus that complements the introductory library research skills unit taught as part of NMSU's English composition courses. Other models for library integration into general orientation courses are found in the sidebar pieces from librarians at Wichita State University and the University of Toledo.

Models for the integration of library skills into freshman seminar courses are provided by library staff at Southwestern University and the University of the Pacific (Parks and Hendrix 1996; Fenske and Clark 1995). Librarians at Southwestern developed library assignments and conducted instructional sessions designed to build upon the texts and themes covered in sections of the Freshman Symposium. For example, a recent assignment had students read one book from a library-developed list having to do with the course's theme, American Culture: Unity and Diversity; find a book review and biographical information on the book's author; and use the information to prepare an oral report and paper for their symposium section (Parks and Hendrix 1996). Because the symposium theme changes each year, library staff members make concerted efforts to bolster their collections in theme areas and develop comprehensive reading lists for the course.

At the University of the Pacific, students participate in a two-semester Mentor Seminar program. The second semester of this program has students investigating societal dilemmas such as global environmental issues, AIDS, cultural diversity, and drug legalization. Students are assigned to research teams covering one of the aforementioned topics and are charged to write a research-based policy paper with an accompanying bibliography on that issue. Library staff members offer a series of workshops focusing on each of the topics in which general research tools (the online catalog, indexes, reference books, etc.) are introduced in a setting that blends demonstration and hands-on practice. Students' library skills are also pre- and posttested to help staff evaluate students' skills and determine what instruction areas need to be reinforced (Fenske and Clark 1995).

In addition to their work with formal courses, it should be noted that librarians are increasingly involved with some of the broader aspects of developing learning communities for first-year students. A spring 1998 discussion on BI-L (Bibliographic Instruction Listserv) elicited postings from librarians in South Carolina, Michigan, Indiana, and Hawaii who reported playing significant roles in helping their institutions plan and assess learning objectives for freshmen and who described freshman programs that included everything from the sponsorship of one-on-one research tutorial sessions in residence halls to the development of linked courses addressing the interplay of information and scholarship.

Just as librarians are responding to broader trends in freshman programming, their outreach efforts also reflect trends in teaching techniques and technologies. Many of the pedagogical focal points of library instruction in the past decade—concept-based instruction, active learning, critical thinking, information literacy, etc.—are evident in contemporary freshman outreach programs. Emily Werrell of Northern Kentucky University (NKU) has written about her staff's involvement with the creation of a variety of library assignments that encourage collaborative learning, selection and evaluation of sources, and some form of final presentation. Care is taken to craft assignments that relate to the issues that students are covering in NKU's UNV 101 course, such as HIV, alcohol and drug addiction, and diversity. Librarians also conduct workshops for UNV 101 instructors in which the assignments and the educational goals behind them are discussed (Werrell 1996). At California State University-San Bernadino, library staff developed an instruction module that features the use of active learning techniques such as librarian-led group discussions and assignments that involve teamwork (Dabbour 1997).

Contemporary library instruction has also been powerfully influenced by technology, as both a teaching tool and a teaching subject. Librarians at California State University-Long Beach employed a quick and upbeat "library infomercial" as a means of motivating students to feel more comfortable using library resources and asking questions—something that is particularly important given the size of their University 100 program (2,000+ students). University of Washington library staff members were key participants in the innovative UWired program, which targets freshmen (and other groups) and integrates teaching, learning, and technology in a number of creative ways. A growing number of librarians at institutions such as Bowling Green State University, California Polytechnic State University, Cornell University, North Carolina State University, and Purdue University have developed online tours and tutorials covering everything from orientation skills to research strategies. Although many of these online tutorials are not directed specifically at first-year students, they emphasize the types of basic research skills typically covered in library instruction for freshman and sophomore students and offer innovations such as randomized questions, automatic feedback, and hyperlinks for quick and easy review of key points. In some cases, such as the *Information Literacy Skills Workbook* used by the University of Wisconsin at Parkside, there is a direct link to a freshman course (Scholz-Crane 1997). Occasionally, such as in the case of the Getting Published project (part of one module of a first-year course at California State University, San Marcos), a well-developed, technology-based program may prove counterproductive within the course framework. Getting Published was discontinued because of the complexity of the sub-ject matter, the students' lack of computer skills, and the determination that, for this purpose and audience, an interactive lecture and exercises were more successful teaching tools than the Web-based program (Sonntag 1999). However, technology will likely continue to serve as a tool for reaching out to large groups of new students who are increasingly computer literate.

Does It Make Any Difference? A Word about Outcomes

> Ultimately the success of our actions on behalf of student learning and retention depends upon the daily actions of all members of the institution, not on the sporadic efforts of a few officially desig-nated members of a retention committee. Properly understood, institutional commitment is the commitment on the part of each and every member of the institution for the welfare, the social and intellectual growth, of all members of the institution (Tinto 1993, 212).

The logical question to follow this discussion of freshman retention pro-grams and the library's role within them is, what works? Or, from the per-spective of those who might view such courses as costly experiments in hand-holding, why bother? Tinto argues that there is "no single path to enhanced student retention, nor promises that all admitted students can be retained" (1993, 212). If this is the case, where is the evidence to support the assertion that freshman courses—and library involvement in such courses—makes any difference?

Since 1980, a number of studies (Upcraft, Finney, and Garland 1984; Chapman and Reed 1987; Fidler and Hunter 1989; Hoff 1996; Henschied 1999) have demonstrated that freshman orientation courses enjoy a posi-tive relationship with student persistence and strengthened academic per-formance. Wilkie and Kuckuck (1989) tracked student participants in Indi-ana University of Pennsylvania's Freshman Seminar who were character-ized as high risk. The authors found that, even in their junior year, student participants' grades were significantly higher, they reported increased use of university resources such as writing services and libraries, and their overall retention rate was 13 percent higher than their counterparts who did not participate in the course. Similarly, Shanley and Witten's 1990 study of University 101 at the University of South Carolina found that over the fifteen-year time span of their study, students who participated in the class had higher sophomore return rates and graduation rates despite the fact that many of these students "were less prepared academically and had a larger proportion of high risk undeclared and minority students than their nonparticipant counterparts" (345). Fidler and Hunter (1989) found that freshman seminar courses can be effective in improving the skills of all types of students, from those with the strongest academic skills to those in need of the most academic assistance. Ketkar and Bennett (1989) found that freshman courses are cost-effective, generating revenue through increased student retention, which more than covers the cost of the course.

Other studies at schools such as Central Missouri State University, Elmhurst College, and the University of Maine have explored and recorded positive outcomes for faculty teaching styles, students' self-perception of abilities, and the behavior of students who are undecided about their majors (Barefoot 1993). In fact, Cuseo notes that "arguably, there may be more empirical research supporting the value of the freshman orientation seminar than for any other single course offered in higher education, simply because traditional courses have never had to document their value empirically" (1991, 3).

It may seem more difficult to link a discrete freshman library experience to long-term student success. However, one general outcome has an important bearing in this regard: the tendency of students who have had a positive introduction to libraries and other campus instructional support units to report higher use of those services throughout their four years (Wilkie and Kuckuck 1989; numerous institutional studies as reported in Fidler and Hunter 1989). It has been well documented by Constance Mellon (1986) and others that students are unlikely to seek help from professors, teaching assistants, or library staff—even when they realize they need it. Levitz and Noel (1989, 74) note that "if we wait for students to come to us, many will fall through the cracks." Other findings touch on outcomes related to everything from the importance of library experiences in promoting the critical thinking skills of first-generation college students (Pascarella 1995) to the impressions of the students themselves. For example, short-term evaluations of the library component for the University of Kansas's Freshman Summer Institute indicated that it was, in many students' estimates, one of the most important aspects of the program. As librarians become more actively involved in projects such as learning communities, there will be additional opportunities to evaluate the effectiveness of a more integrated approach to the development of information literacy skills among first-year students. Clearly, there is a need for more research into the effectiveness of library instruction programs and it will become increasingly important for librarians to engage in the assessment of their instructional outreach both during and beyond the first year (Lindauer 1998; Pausch and Popp 1999).

Clearly, libraries also stand to benefit from these outreach efforts. As stated in Gardner, Decker, and McNairy, "the Freshman Year Experience programs involve a partnership of faculty, academic administrators, students personnel administrators, library administrators, and faculty librarians. Such programs recognize the total development of freshmen: academic, vocational, personal, social" (1986, 159). The development of these critical partnerships allows academic library staff to become a more visible and critical part of their institution's work with promoting student success. And academic libraries—like the larger institutions of which they are a part—stand to benefit from any studies that help us to understand our patrons (in this case, students) and their needs. Whether data are collected informally through general observations at the reference desk or formally through literature reviews and pretesting of students, librarians who are able to base services on a stronger understanding of their users are better equipped to ensure that their efforts are useful—and even integral—to fostering student success.

References

Adkinson, K. 1996. Evaluation of the 1995 Freshman Summer Institute. Master's thesis, University of Kansas.

Baber, C. P. 1928. Freshman courses in the use of the library. *Library Journal* 53:1041–42.

Barefoot, B. 1993. *Exploring the Evidence: Reporting Outcomes of Freshman Seminars.* Columbia, S.C.: National Resource Center for the Freshman Year Experience.

Barkley, M. 1939. Arrows for freshmen. *Library Journal* 64:402–4.

Braxton, J. M., A. Sullivan, and R. M. Johnson. 1997. Appraising Tinto's theory of college student departure. In vol. 12 of *Higher Education: Handbook of Theory and Research*, ed. J. Smart. New York: Agathon Press.

Braxton, J. M., N. Vesper, and D. Hossler. 1995. Expectations for college and student persistence. *Research in Higher Education* 36(4):595–612.

Brubacher, J., and W. Rudy. 1997. Reintegration of curriculum and extracurriculum and the university transformed, 1975–1995. In *Higher Education in Transition: A History of American Colleges and Universities.* New Brunswick, N.J.: Transaction Publishers.

Chapman, L. C., and P. J. Reed. 1987. Evaluating the effectiveness of a freshman orientation course. *Journal of College Student Personnel* 28(2):178–79.

Consortium for Student Retention Data Exchange (CSRDE). 2000. Retention and graduation rates in 294 colleges and universities. Available from http://www.occe.ou.edu/CSRDE/; INTERNET.

Cuseo, J. 1991. *The Freshman Orientation Seminar: A Research-based Rationale for its Value, Delivery, and Content.* ERIC, ED 334883.

Dabbour, K. 1997. Applying active learning methods to the design of library instruction for a freshman seminar. *College & Research Libraries* 58:299–307.

Drury, F. K. W. 1928. Library orientation of freshman students. *Library Journal* 53:1023–25.

Eldridge, B. L. 1928. An experiment in library instruction for college freshmen. *Library Journal* 53:986–88.

English, A. J. 1926. How shall we instruct the freshmen in the use of the library? *School & Society* 24:779–85.

Erickson, E. W. 1949. Library instruction in the freshman orientation program. *College and Research Libraries* 10:445–48.

Fenske, R., and S. Clark. 1995. Incorporating library instruction in a general education program for college freshmen. *Reference Services Review* 23:69–74.

Fidler, P., and M. Hunter. 1989. How seminars enhance student success. In *The Freshman Year Experience: Helping Students Survive and Succeed in College*, ed. M. L. Upcraft, John N. Gardner, and associates. San Francisco: Jossey-Bass.

Fitts, C. T., and F. H. Swift. 1928. *The Construction of Orientation Courses for College Freshmen*. Berkeley, Calif.: University of California Press.

Gardner, J., D. Decker, and F. McNairy. 1986. Taking the library to freshmen students via the freshman seminar concept. *Advances in Library Administration and Organization* 6:153–171.

Gordon, V. P. 1989. Origins and purposes of the freshman seminar. In *The Freshman Year Experience: Helping Students Survive and Succeed in College*, ed. M. L. Upcraft, J. N. Gardner, and associates. San Francisco: Jossey-Bass.

Hartz, Frederic R. 1964. Freshman library orientation: A re-evaluation. *Improving College and University Teaching* 12:78–80.

Henscheid, J. M. 1999. Washington State University freshman seminar program research findings. Available from http://salc.wsu.edu/fr_seminar/research_findings.asp; INTERNET. Link no longer valid.

Hoff, M. P. 1996. The first five years of freshman seminars at Dalton College: Student success and retention. *Journal of the Freshman Year Experience and Students in Transition* 8:33–42.

James, A. E. 1941. Freshmen and the library. *Wilson Library Bulletin* 15:403–7.

Jewler, A. J. 1989. Elements of an effective seminar: The University 101 program. In *The Freshman Year Experience: Helping Students Survive and Succeed in College*, ed. M. L. Upcraft, J. N. Gardner, and associates. San Francisco: Jossey-Bass.

Jordan, D. S. 1910. The care and culture of freshmen. *North American Review* 191:441–48.

Kelly, M. C. 1995. Student retention and academic libraries. *College & Research Libraries News* 11:757–59.

Ketkar, K., and S. D. Bennett. 1989. Strategies for evaluating a freshman studies program. *Journal of the Freshman Year Experience* 1:33–44.

Levine, A. 1978. *Handbook on Undergraduate Curriculum*. San Francisco: Jossey-Bass.

———. 1998. *When Hope and Fear Collide: A Portrait of Today's College Student*. San Francisco: Jossey-Bass.

Levitz, R., and L. Noel. 1989. Connecting students to institutions: Keys to retention and success. In *The Freshman Year Experience: Helping Students Survive and Succeed in College*, ed. M. L. Upcraft, J. N. Gardner, and associates. San Francisco: Jossey-Bass.

Levitz, R., L. Noel, and B. J. Richter. 1999. Strategic moves for retention success. In *Promising Practices in Recruitment, Remediation, and Retention*, ed. G. H. Gaither. San Francisco: Jossey Bass.

Lindauer, B. G. 1998. Defining and measuring the library's impact on campuswide outcomes. *College & Research Libraries* 59:546–70.

Little, E. A. 1936. *Instruction in the Use of Books and Libraries in Colleges and Universities*. Ann Arbor, Mich.: University of Michigan Libraries.

McCoy, Ralph E. 1962. Automation in freshman library instruction. *Wilson Library*

Bulletin 36:468–72.

Marteena, C. H. 1956. Library orientation for college freshmen based on reference 'R' outline. *Library Journal* 81:1226–28.

Mellon, C. 1986. Library anxiety: A grounded theory and its development. *College & Research Libraries* 47:160–65.

Merritt, G. 1956. Library orientation for college freshmen in the small college during orientation week. *Library Journal* 81:1224–25.

Meyering, H. R., and S. Pierson. 1939. Introducing the library to college students. *Journal of Higher Education* 10:447–49.

National Resource Center for the Freshman Year Experience & Students in Transition. 2000. Available from http://www.sc.edu/fye; INTERNET.

Newsome, M. E. 1940. A library course for freshmen. *Wilson Library Bulletin* 15: 338.

Noel, L. 1985. Increasing student retention: New challenges and potential. In *Increasing Student Retention,* ed. L. Noel, R. Levitz, D. Saluri, & associates. San Francisco: Jossey-Bass.

Noel Levitz. 2000. Available from http://noellevitz.com; INTERNET.

Parks, J., and D. Hendrix. 1996. Integrating library instruction into the curriculum through freshman symposium. *Reference Services Review* 24:65–72.

Pascarella, E. T. 1995. *What Have We Learned From the First Year of the National Study of Student Learning?* ERIC, ED 381054.

Pascarella, E. T., and P. Terenzini. 1983. Predicting voluntary freshman year persistence/withdrawal behavior in a residential university: A path analytic validation of the Tinto model. *Journal of Educational Psychology* 52(2):60–75.

Pausch, L. M., and M. P. Popp. 1999. Assessment of information literacy: Lessons from the higher education assessment movement. Paper presented at the 9th National Conference of the Association of College & Research Libraries, Detroit, April 8–11, 1999. Available from http://www.ala.org/acrl/paperhtm/d30.html; INTERNET.

Salony, Mary F. 1995. History of bibliographic instruction: Changing trends from books to the electronic world. In *Library Instruction Revisited: Bibliographic Instruction Comes of Age,* edited by Lynne M. Martin. Binghamton, N.Y.: Haworth.

Scholz-Crane, A. 1997. Web-based instruction resources. Available from http://crab.rutgers.edu/~scholzcr/cil/libexp.html; INTERNET. Link no longer valid.

Sellers, R. Z. 1950. What shall we do for freshmen? *Wilson Library Bulletin* 24:360–65.

Shanley, M., and C. Witten. 1990. University 101 freshman seminar course: A longitudinal study of persistence, retention, and graduation rates. *NASPA Journal* 27:344–52.

Smith, Ada Jeannette. 1926.

Sonntag, G. 1999. Using technology in a first year experience course. *College & Undergraduate Libraries* 6:1–17.

Stage, F. 1989. Reciprocal effects between the academic and social integration of college students. *Research in Higher Education* 30:517–30.

A Student success story: Freshman interest groups at the University of Missouri-Columbia. 1996. *Student Life Studies Abstracts* 1:1–4.

Tinto, V. 1993. *Leaving College: Rethinking the Causes and Cures of Student Attrition.* Chicago: University of Chicago Press.

———. 1997. Colleges as communities: Exploring the educational character of student persistence. *Journal of Higher Education* 68(6):599–623.

———. 1998. Colleges as communities: Taking research on student persistence seriously. *Review of Higher Education* 21(2):167–77.

Tinto, V., and A. Goodsell. 1993. *Freshman Interest Groups and the First Year Experience: Constructing Student Communities in a Large University.* ERIC, ED 358778.

Upcraft, M. L., J. E. Finney, and P. Garland. 1984. Orientation: A context. In *Orienting Students to College*, ed. M. L Upcraft. San Francisco: Jossey-Bass.

University of Washington. n.d. *The Future is Here: Teaching, Learning, Technology* [brochure describing UWired project].

Ury, C., and T. King. 1995. Reinforcement of library orientation instruction for freshman seminar students. *Research Strategies* 13:153–64.

Vesey, L. R. 1965. *The Emergence of the American University.* Chicago: University of Chicago Press, 121–79.

Wakiji, E., and J. Thomas. 1997. MTV to the rescue: Changing library attitudes through video. *College & Research Libraries* 58:211–16.

Werrell, E. 1996. The freshman year experience: A library component that works. In *Programs That Work: Papers and Session Materials Presented at the 24th National LOEX Library Instruction Conference.* Ann Arbor, Mich.: Pierian.

White, C. M. 1937. Freshmen and the library. *Journal of Higher Education* 8:39–42.

Wilkie, C., and S. Kuckuck. 1989. A longitudinal study of the effects of a freshman seminar. *Journal of the Freshman Year Experience* 1:7–16.

Wingspread Group on Higher Education. 1993. *An American Imperative: Higher Expectations for Higher Education.* Racine, Wisc.: Johnson Foundation.

Young, A. B. 1937. The freshmen—our opportunity. *Library Journal* 62:235–36.

Zeller, Rose C. 1950. What shall we do for our freshmen? *Wilson Library Bulletin* 24:360–65.

Authors' Note

Information about many of the programs mentioned in this chapter was obtained from secondary sources and follow-up checks on the home pages of those institutions.

The Role of the Library in Student Retention

Darla Rushing and Deborah Poole

Introduction

The role of the library in student retention has been an occasional topic of discussion in the library literature since Kramer and Kramer's 1968 groundbreaking study at California State Polytechnic College in the mid-1960s. The impetus for that early study was a call for accountability from the state legislature that expressed growing concerns about students' failure to persist. Over the past quarter century, accountability has been taken up in state legislatures across the country. In private higher education, retention of students has become a major issue that has spawned an entire culture of retention experts and enrollment managers. Economic as well as educational issues are at stake for both institutions and the students they serve.

Where does the library fit in this complex scenario? Maurie Caitlin Kelly has called for academic libraries and librarians to play pivotal roles in both the education and the retention of students. She argues that libraries are an integral part of the college experience and that it is vital for librarians to participate in campuswide programs to promote this ideal. Furthermore, she suggests that librarians should be proactive in learning about student behaviors and in developing and participating in retention programs at the institutional level—in short, they should get involved (Kelly 1995).

This discussion of the role of the library in student retention is multifaceted. It outlines the involvement of one library in strategic planning at the university level. It also documents the authors' research on the positive impact of library employment on students' persistence and the resultant recognition of the library's importance to campuswide retention efforts. Finally, it suggests that there is great potential to develop a cadre of "library alumni" who, because of their belief in the importance of the library in the educational mission, are prepared to play major roles to support the library within the institution.

Getting Involved: Planning and Student Retention

Loyola University New Orleans is at once typical and, as every private liberal arts university attempts to be, unique. It is rightly proud of its place, since 1990, on *U.S. News & World Report's* list of top regional universities

The authors wish to thank Stephen Bertram, MLIS, technical services assistant, for his documentation of work-study employment in the cataloging department at the Monroe Library.

and colleges in the United States.[1] Uniquely, Loyola prospered for nearly a century as a Catholic university in the most Catholic city in America, a prosperity guaranteed by a continuous supply of well-qualified students coming primarily from parochial school backgrounds. Founded in 1837 as the College of the Immaculate Conception, Loyola had roots in the community that were deep and strong. Its students were highly motivated, if not all affluent.[2] Typically, as private higher education became more expensive, especially when compared with nearby state universities, and as fewer students came out of the parochial school tradition, Loyola crashed into the wall of college-age demography with the same force as other private colleges and universities throughout the nation.

By 1995, Loyola found itself in an enrollment crisis and the university's new president and other strategic planners began to see recruitment as only one part of the picture. Retention was tracked for several previous years, and, to its dismay, the university administration discovered that entering freshmen persisted to graduation in four years at rates ranging from 31 to 38 percent. The rates of students graduating in five or six years ranged from 48 to 56 percent (Loyola University New Orleans 2000). The entire university community was stunned by these numbers because it believed that Loyola was providing a high-quality, student-centered environment that nurtured its students both academically and personally.

The library faculty might not have been aware of the magnitude of the retention crisis if they had not been actively participating at the highest levels of university planning. During the 1980s, the library faculty began an aggressive campaign to seek membership on key university committees. Planning for a new library building began in the late 1970s and culminated in the *Final Report of the Blue Ribbon Task Force for the Library's Academic Future* (Loyola University New Orleans 1988), but it was not until 1988 that the director (now dean) of the library became an ex officio member of the university planning team (UPT). In 1992, a library faculty member was added to the UPT, joining other faculty representatives from the various colleges. For two years, the library's faculty representative to the university planning team served by appointment of the university president on the steering committee of the UPT. The steering committee is made up of the president, the provost, the associate vice-presidents for Academic Affairs and Student Affairs, and two faculty members.

In addition to strategic planning, the library faculty were involved in institutional assessment. During Loyola's last re-accreditation review by the Southern Association of Colleges and Schools, librarians were members of eight of the thirteen self-study committees and chairs of two of them. The librarian who chaired the Financial Resources Committee was subsequently elected by the University Senate to membership on the University Budget Committee and was appointed by the university president to a term on the steering committee of the University Budget Committee.

The involvement of the dean of libraries and library faculty in strategic planning made the entire library faculty and staff acutely aware of the significance of retention. The up-close-and-personal look at the university's finances brought into grim reality the economic consequences of students' failure to persist. Engagement in institutional planning and assessment motivated the library faculty to reflect upon the library's impact on student recruitment and retention, and therefore student success.

Getting Involved: A Work-Study Model for Student Retention Success

Discovery is an interesting and often serendipitous process, no less so in the library world than in the scientific. The case study presented here documents a microcosm of retention success in one library's work-study program. It also illustrates how, over time, the library has become a major player in the university's retention program and has created a new vision of the library's centrality to the university. The discovery that working in the library supports student success has been particularly rewarding for the library faculty and staff.

The lower-than-expected graduation rates for Loyola students did not seem to reflect the library's experience with its employees who were participating in the federal work-study program. However, we had never thought to formally study whether the students in this program were more successful than the average student. In order to see whether our intuitive experience could be documented, the library's Cataloging Department did a retrospective study of those students who had been our work-study employees. The supervisor of student workers had kept records, beginning in 1986, of every student who had worked for at least one semester in the department. There were fifty-two students whose dates of entering the university plus six years placed them in our experiential group. We discovered that thirty-two of those students (61.5%) had graduated, all in four years or four years plus a semester. This graduation rate was significantly higher than the university's four-year average of 31 to 38 percent. We knew the circumstances surrounding the departure from Loyola of all but one of the remaining twenty students.

Particularly noteworthy was the performance of the minority group, who graduated from Loyola at a rate of 65 percent. Of ten African American students, eight graduated; of five Hispanic Americans, four graduated; of six Asian Americans, one graduated.[3] The success of the department's minority group is contraindicated generally, particularly for students who are perceived to be at risk because of economic factors.

Serendipitous discovery or planned outcome? We began to think about what had created this microcosm of success, if it were not simply a statistical anomaly that often occurs with small experimental groups. Stanley Wilder suggests that library employment can be a strong incentive to academic success, and therefore retention. Wilder (1990, 1037) outlines the "natural advantages of the library job":

- Library jobs demystify the library. For students who would otherwise feel intimidated by the library, daily contact reduces anxiety and may produce a positive predisposition to further use.
- There may be a benefit to physically placing at-risk students in a study-related environment, in close contact with good academic role models.
- Library work naturally exposes students to materials that can be useful in completing course work.

Our experience in examining the relationship between library work-study and retention confirms Wilder's thesis.

Library student employees had always been essential at Loyola, rather than superfluous, and the work-study program was never "make-work" in the library. Then, in the 1980s, the university reduced staff size and all departments in the library began to rely more heavily on student employees. In the Cataloging Department, an average of eight to ten students per semester performed nearly all of the department's clerical and processing tasks. As the tasks became increasingly complex, so did the training requirements, which increased the amount of faculty and staff time required for training. This was particularly frustrating because the department experienced an enormously high student turnover rate from semester to semester and year to year.

In exit interviews with students who transferred from the Cataloging Department to other departments on campus or within the library, the reasons for leaving included statements such as: "I never get to study on the job like my friends do in the [other campus] department"; "the work is repetitious and boring" or, alternatively, "the work is too difficult"; "I want to find a job where I have more contact with people"; and, finally, and perhaps most understandably from the career perspective, "I want to transfer to the department of my major." To stem the tide of constant turnover, the Cataloging Department set a departmental goal of 100 percent retention from first semester to second and from freshman to sophomore year and developed a program for "keeping them happy, keeping them working, and keeping them working happily."

The first step was to improve hiring procedures. Rather than accepting every student sent by the student financial aid office, we began conducting interviews that included questions about students' preferences, interests, availability to work during the department's hours of operation, previous work experience, library experiences, and computer and language skills. Most often, students had no previous work experience other than fast food or retail. We described the kinds of jobs to be done in the department, from computer work in OCLC to the manual processing of books, emphasizing the importance of the student's potential position to the library and to the university. Usually, this discussion of our needs vis-à-vis the student's needs resulted in a mutually agreeable decision that the student would or would not work in the Cataloging Department. Over time, we have come to believe that it is important, especially when dealing with first-year students, to treat the work-study interview as an opportunity to guide students to jobs that will contribute to their integration into the fabric of the university community. The work-study award is guaranteed, but the right fit of each student to his or her actual campus job should be negotiable by both the student and the department.

Our second step was to begin a tradition of "fall convocation," a meeting required of everyone in the department: library faculty, staff, and students. Conveniently, Loyola has what it calls a window in the schedule (12:30 P.M. to 2:00 P.M., Tuesdays and Thursdays) that allows students and faculty time for meetings, community activities, and socializing. The Cataloging Department's convocation has given everyone an opportunity to meet and socialize. It also has presented us with a chance to talk once more about the library's mission and the students' place in it, to explain and review departmental rules and regulations, and to remind students of the advantages of working in the library.

As the return rate for our student employees began to improve, we transferred training responsibilities for first-year students from staff to upper-level students. Although a library faculty or staff member provided the initial instruction, upper-level students handled detailed follow-up and ongoing training. The obvious benefits to the department were that staff time was saved, the returning students enjoyed their roles as trainers, and the first-year students felt less intimidated by people who, perhaps only a year earlier, had been where they now were.

In our convocation and in daily work throughout the year, we emphasized to the students the seriousness, the real-job nature of their work, and reminded them of the transferability of the skills they were learning. This reinforcement was formalized by mid-semester performance evaluations that took place in fall and spring. In the convocation, we also discussed our potential value as references for employment outside the university and for graduate and professional schools. In fact, a primary reason for our having kept student records was that we occasionally received calls for references years after the students had left and we wanted to have some corporate memory of each student.

Although we emphasized the importance of the work, we realized that better retention for the department meant making work not only important, but also enjoyable. Many retention experts have noted that social integration—the fun of college—is as important as perceptions of the academic quality of the institution in students' tendency to persist. Recognizing that our work-study students spent fifteen to twenty hours per week doing highly skilled work, we decided that, for those activities that did not require total concentration, such as book processing, we would allow a certain amount of socializing. For more complex tasks (computer work, for example), we allowed headphones. To relieve boredom, we trained each student to do a variety of tasks and assigned work according to the individual student's abilities and preferences. We gave a great deal of attention to distributing all tasks fairly (Young 1998).

A less formal atmosphere has provided a better sense of community in the Cataloging Department. Other benefits have included opportunities for cross-cultural friendships among students, which probably would not have happened in any other setting with the possible exception of the Honors Program or team sports. Students have felt free to discuss academic problems with each other and with the staff. Occasionally, they have talked about behaviors that might threaten their academic success or be physically dangerous to themselves or others. Over time, this informal atmosphere has enabled library faculty and staff to intervene or to offer help with both academic and personal problems that might cause students to drop out of the university. It is our practice to direct a student to an advisor, an associate dean, a faculty member we know to be particularly sympathetic, or a counselor in the Division of Student Affairs.

During the twelve-year period that encompassed our study, the departmental return rate improved dramatically, so that we now have students who work in the library's Cataloging Department for their entire university careers. Without claiming its ultimate importance as an incentive, we believe that, where students are concerned, food is good. The annual convocation includes lunch provided by the library faculty and staff and has become a time when the upper-level students demand their favorite foods. At the end of each semester, we have lunch or dinner at the home of a library faculty or staff member. These official parties are supplemented by other social events throughout the year to which library faculty and staff invite students. The ultimate reward for graduation from the Cataloging Department—working from matriculation to graduation—is dinner at a restaurant of the student's choice hosted by the department head. There is no financial support from the library or from the university for entertainment, but there is release time for these events.

We reported our case study to the university planning team, which drew attention to the library's potential to contribute significantly to the university's retention efforts. What began as an attempt to reduce turnover in our work-study program resulted in the creation of an atmosphere that fosters connectedness and a place where true mentoring occurs. The ultimate result has been student persistence and student success.

Getting Involved: Students and the New Library

A popular and widely circulated e-mail message from Beloit College's Class of 2004 Mindset List notes that for students entering college in fall 2000, "there have always been ATM machines" and "they have always bought telephones rather than rent them from AT&T" (Nief 2000). Who better to design the library of the twenty-first century than students?

During the planning phase for the new building, the dean of libraries sought input from the Student Library Advisory Committee through regular meetings with that group, and librarians conducted surveys and focus groups with other students. Through these conversations, we learned that students envisioned the new library to be a cross between a Barnes & Noble and a favorite coffeehouse. The cappuccino machine idea has not materialized, but there is a student lounge with vending machines in the center of the new library and we sell spill-proof travel mugs that sport the library's logo. Students also said that they needed and wanted places to study in groups, and the new Monroe Library provides such spaces. Though some may say that all a student will need in the new millennium is a good computer and a fast network connection, students continue to say that they value the library as a place. The design and furnishings of the Monroe Library balance students' needs for community and collaborative learning with quiet study and reflection.

Like other academic libraries, we have allied ourselves with our campus computing unit, the Office of Information Technology (IT). The new library building was planned to incorporate selected IT staff and three twenty-four-hour computer labs that accommodate twenty-six-students in each lab. The library and IT have established a working group to review, develop, and support further collaboration in providing services to our users.

Getting Involved: Student Learning

The Monroe Library has a strong commitment to instruction. The library took an early lead in teaching Internet-related classes to the Loyola community. The instruction program includes workshops on Web page creation, scanning and PowerPoint presentation development, and Internet-based research sessions in business, science, the humanities, and the social sciences. These workshops have brought the library much acclaim and a high level of visibility in the university. Library faculty work closely with teaching faculty to develop curriculum-related instruction sessions, resources for courses, and Web pages, all designed with the student in mind.

Although much of our time and energy have been devoted to the excitement of the Internet, we nevertheless have given attention to students who might be perceived as at risk. We have collaborated with the Office of International Student Affairs and the Office of Academic Enrichment, which provides a broad range of academic support services. The library prepares workshops tailored to specific needs that help overcome barriers of language, culture, or disability. Mary L. Smalls advises academic libraries to prepare "a caring and sensitive environment for students to learn. Such an environment lends itself to retaining students who feel less frustrated and more self-assured of their academic purpose" (1987, 7). Historically, the library at Loyola has made the creation of such an environment a high priority.

The Peer Information Counseling (PIC) program makes using the library a positive experience for all students, but especially minority students.

Modeled on the PIC program developed at the University of Michigan Undergraduate Library (MacAdam and Nichols 1989), Loyola's program was one of the first in the region. Academically successful minority students are hired as reference assistants and given extensive training to work at the reference desk. Their presence often invites students to ask for help when they might be reluctant to bother or interrupt a librarian or to appear silly or ignorant but would feel comfortable asking a fellow student for assistance. The PIC students are an essential part of our reference service (Simonsen 1996).

Getting Involved: Partnerships with Academic and Student Affairs

The trend in higher education throughout the 1990s regarding freshman orientation was to more closely integrate academic and student life. At Loyola, as responsibility for orientation moved from Academic Affairs (Admissions) to Student Affairs, a New Student Orientation Committee was founded with a strong library faculty presence. This committee formalized the library's role in orientation programs and provided an entrée into helping coordinate orientation efforts on campus.

The library participates in summer and fall orientations and at campus fairs for new students and their parents. These occasions provide opportunities to meet and greet students, promote the services of the library, and recruit students for library employment. At other times during the year, the library participates in the Office of Admission's recruitment programs for senior high school students, such as the President's Open House and the Black Student Experience.

By 1998, the library was poised to take a major role in the university's retention effort. Our documented successes with work-study students and peer learning and our partnerships with Admissions and Student Affairs made the library a logical point of integration for retention initiatives. The university prepared to capitalize on the promise of the new library as a recruitment and retention tool and, significantly, as a central place where those initiatives would be realized.

Getting Involved: The University Task Force on Student Success and Retention

When retention became the number one priority for the university, the associate vice-president for Academic Affairs formed the Student Retention Task Force with the goal of completely integrating the academic and student affairs divisions of the university in the retention mission. The initial task force included the associate vice-president for Academic Affairs, the dean of Admissions, the director of Institutional Research, and the associate vice-president for Student Affairs, as well as staff from these units. The associate deans of the colleges and six faculty members, including the authors, completed the membership.

The entire task force attended a national conference on student retention sponsored by USA Group Noel-Levitz. Noel-Levitz, a private company that markets educational services, is a national leader in recruitment and retention consulting for higher education. Loyola began using the Noel-Levitz Student Satisfaction Inventory™ in 1998. This survey, given to nearly a thousand Loyola students annually, continues to provide the university with a means of learning what is important to our students—what factors might contribute to their satisfaction and therefore retention—and also what is less important. The relative levels of importance are measured against satisfaction, with the result that the institution has a better understanding of what makes students stay or leave.

The importance of the retention effort led administrators to expand the membership of the task force to 120 faculty, students, alumni, staff, and administrators who were charged with developing a university-wide plan including action strategies, implementation plans, and clear measures of the university's progress toward improving the quality of student life and learning. In a SWOT (strengths, weaknesses, opportunities, threats) analysis, the task force identified Loyola's new J. Edgar and Louise S. Monroe Library as a major internal strength.

The task force was divided into ten work groups focusing on key areas of campus life. The authors were participants in three groups: academic support and career development, freshman experience, and freshman learning communities. Among the action strategies recommended by the task force and adopted by the university planning team was the creation of the Center for Academic and Career Excellence. Centrally located on the first floor of Loyola's new Monroe Library, the ACE Center, as it has come to be known, is a cooperative effort among eight university services that have joined together to provide one location for students seeking information, career guidance, and tutoring in all academic areas. Student assistants from the various services staff the ACE Center. The library's peer information counselors, who are trained to give particular attention to the information needs of minority students, staff the ACE Center as well as the library's reference desk.

Staying Involved: Keeping Up with "Library Alumni"

All of our experiences, both administrative and educational, have taught us the importance of assessment. The usefulness of the student employment study has motivated the library to begin tracking student employees in all areas and to consciously think in terms of retention—retention not simply for the good of the library, but also for the good of the student. Loyola University New Orleans is committed to turning its freshmen into graduates. The Student Retention Task Force will guide all units of the university in this enterprise, and the library will play a major role.

Connectedness to the institution is seen as the most important factor in student retention. The Cataloging Department's experience caused the library to realize that all of our work-study students spend more contact hours a week with library faculty and staff than with teaching faculty until perhaps their senior year. This contact provides opportunities for librarians to influence the lives of many students and thus makes an understanding of that reality and all its implications imperative.

Perhaps the most notable opportunity is the potential for recruiting library and information professionals, "library majors," if you will. Because work-study itself provides an opportunity for many minority students, there is an added potential for minority recruitment to the profession. Three of the thirty-two graduates who worked in the Cataloging Department are now librarians, our professional colleagues. The first library alumna is a minority female who, after earning both library and law degrees on full-tuition scholarships, is now employed by Lexis-Nexis. Another is now an archivist at the University of Minnesota, and a third is a manager in library support services at OCLC.

At Loyola, we have come to view the education of our student employees as a large part of our teaching mission. We teach them how to function in a work environment, while they simultaneously learn what they need to know academically to prepare themselves for their careers. Learning how to succeed in the workplace is probably as important as anything else they learn at the university.

The professional relationships and friendships made with library faculty and staff and with other students have fostered another kind of community as well. Our former work-study students have become true library alumni. In our capital campaign for the library, even very recent graduates who are strapped with student loans have made gifts to the library building and endowment funds. As libraries become more dependent on philanthropic gifts to supplement operating budgets, librarians should be cultivating their library alumni.

Finally, we want our students to be lifelong learners as well as lifelong appreciators of what libraries can do for individuals and communities. We have opportunities to do this every day in the various contexts in which we meet students. Mark Sutton, the library's former head of reference, once stated, "I will have considered myself a success as an academic librarian if one of my students sits on a library board in his or her community." Loyola's board of trustees has recently appointed two new young members, one a former work-study student and one a former member of the Student Library Advisory Committee, to the Library Visiting Committee. The Visiting Committee is charged with the promotion and development of the Monroe Library and plays a key role in fund-raising initiatives. This is only the beginning of what we hope will be a fully developed program of staying involved with students whose contact with the library fosters their continued support for and interest in the library.

Notes

1. Currently, Loyola is in seventh place regionally. See 2001 college rankings (2000).
2. A thinly veiled fictional account of what Loyola looked like to a New Orleans "downtowner" freshman in the 1950s can be found in Ignatius D'Aquila's *Remembering Dixie*. New Orleans: Hot August Nights, 1997, p. 23ff.
3. We would ordinarily expect the Asian American retention rate to be high. In our particular group, the five Asian Americans who did not graduate transferred to other institutions to pursue engineering degrees that Loyola does not offer.

References

2001 college rankings: Southern universities top schools. 2000. *Online U.S. News*, 11 November. Available from http://www.usnews.com/usnews/edu/college/rankings/sthunivs/sthu_a2.htm; INTERNET. Link no longer valid.

Kelly, Maurie Caitlin. 1995. Student retention and academic libraries. *College & Research Libraries News* 56(11):757-59.

Kramer, Lloyd A., and Martha B. Kramer. 1968. The college library and the dropout. *College and Research Libraries* 29 (July):310.

Loyola University New Orleans Office of Institutional Research. 2000. *Loyola University New Orleans Graduation Rate*. April 5.

Loyola University New Orleans. (1988). *Final Report of the Blue Ribbon Task Force for the Library's Academic Future*.

MacAdam, Barbara, and Darlene P. Nichols. 1989. Peer information counseling: An academic library program for minority students. *Journal of Academic Librarianship* 15(4):204-9.

Nief, Ron. 2000. Beloit College releases the class of 2004 mindset list [cited 31 August 2000]. Available from http://www.beloit.edu/~pubaff/releases/Mindset-List-2004.html; INTERNET.

Simonsen, Doreen. 1996. Talent, knowledge, and service: Student library experts at the reference desk. *Loyola University Library News*, no. 21 (winter):1-2, 6.

Smalls, Mary L. 1987. The role of the academic library and faculty in the retention of black students in higher education. Paper presented at the Third National Conference on Black Student Retention in Higher Education, Tampa, Fla., 3 November. ERIC, ED 304059.

Wilder, Stanley. 1990. Library jobs and student retention. *College & Research Libraries News* 51(11):1037.

Young, Sherry E. 1998. Making federal work-study work. *College & Research Libraries News* 59(7):490-92, 525.

The Penn State Engineering Library and Women in Engineering Program:
A Partnership to Encourage the Retention of Women Engineering Students

Kelly M. Jordan

> Through outreach programs, colleges can make an enormous im-
> pact on young women's attitudes towards the engineering profes-
> sion..." –Eleanor Baum

Excerpt from Baum's "Recruiting and Graduating Women: The Underrepresented Student"
article that appeared in the December 1990 *IEEE Communications Magazine*

Introduction

In the United States, women comprise approximately 20 percent of the
total undergraduate engineering population (Engineering Workforce Commission 1997). In an effort to meet their own needs for a more diversified
workforce, potential employers are demanding that colleges and universities produce more women engineers. As a result, an increasingly intensified
effort has begun to recruit and retain these students.

> Penn State Women in Engineering Program (WEP)
> For more information about the program, contact Director Barbara
> Bogue. http://www.engr.psu.edu/WEP

At Pennsylvania State University, the Women in Engineering Program
(WEP) spearheads the university's recruitment and retention efforts. The
WEP uses a variety of activities to encourage women to enter engineering at
Penn State, including a summer camp for older Girl Scouts, where they
learn about engineering and do fun building projects; special overnight
events, where prospective students stay with women engineering students;
and one-on-one sessions with the director of the WEP in which students
can ask questions about engineering and Penn State.

Even with special recruitment efforts, retention remains a big challenge. At Penn State and other universities, approximately half of the women
enrolled in engineering programs change majors (Astin 1993). Some change
majors after they realize they do not enjoy studying engineering; others cite
more troubling causes such as the isolation of being a woman in predomi-
nantly male classrooms, the lack of positive female engineering role mod-

els, and feelings of overall inferiority and as high achievers in high school now receiving average grades in engineering (Lazarus 1996; Takahira and Goodings 1998; Taylor 1997). These factors, which are prevalent at many universities, including Penn State, can often be combated through a positive support system. Thus, the creation of a support system is a primary focus of the WEP.

To this end, the WEP has created special programs geared toward encouraging women to believe that they can—and should—stay in engineering. Some of the programs are academic in nature, such as those designed to increase the skill level of students in specific courses within the engineering curriculum. Other programs have more of a social emphasis, such as the mentoring program that matches students with women who are Penn State engineering alumnae or upper level engineering students. Additional activities of the WEP include orientations for first-year students, tutoring, special lectures, project courses, collaborations with individual engineering departments, and workshops that emphasize hands-on skills and career development.

The Engineering Library and Women in Engineering Program Collaboration

The idea that a positive support system will encourage women students to stay in engineering is also the motivating factor behind the collaboration of the engineering library and the WEP. The collaboration is centered on the idea that the two groups should team up to create an information support system for women engineering students.

> **Penn State Chapter of the Society of Women Engineers**
> http://www.engr.psu.edu/SWE
> Provides information on the chapter programs and activities.
>
> **Society of Women Engineers**
> http://www.swe.org
> The national Web site.

One librarian in the engineering library is designated as a contact person for women engineering students. Students can go to that librarian (in this case, the engineering reference librarian) for extra research help and to get answers to their specific questions about the field of engineering and issues related to women engineers. Creating an environment in which students can get answers to their questions and solutions to their research problems helps them complete their assignments, increases their confidence in their ability to do engineering course work, and perhaps factors into their decision to stay in the program. The engineering library and the WEP have identified three areas that are central to achieving this goal: outreach, collection development, and special joint projects.

Outreach

Outreach is the most important component of the collaboration because an effective information support system relies on making contact with as many women engineering students as possible. This is accomplished in four ways: the Penn State student chapter of the Society of Women Engineers, a women in engineering student listserv, a referral system with the WEP, and the Women in Engineering Program orientation.

The student chapter of the Society of Women Engineers is one of the largest, most active clubs on the Penn State campus. The group holds several meetings throughout the year. At the first meeting of the fall semester, a presentation is made by the engineering reference librarian that details what the engineering library can do to help the students. This early contact has proved to be very beneficial. Throughout the school year, women engineering students come into the Engineering library looking for assistance, often recalling the assistance that was offered at the meeting. It goes to show that students never forget an offer to help!

The WEP listserv reaches the e-mail accounts of all the undergraduate women engineering students at Penn State. This is a very popular means of communication between the students and the WEP. The engineering library also uses the listserv. At various times during the semester, the engineering reference librarian post messages to advertise library instruction seminars and to offer research help. These postings are always met with e-mails from students who are interested in taking the seminars and from those who have questions regarding their research.

Another component of the outreach effort is the referral system with the WEP. Not only does the WEP serve as a recruitment and retention office, but its staff functions as unofficial guidance counselors for women engineering students, helping them with any problems they are having with classes or adjusting to college life. Occasionally, they encounter students who are having problems completing their research assignments and refer them to the engineering library. Conversely, when the engineering reference librarian encounters students who are having problems with their classes, or those who are considering dropping out of the engineering program, the women are referred to the WEP for assistance. This referral program has worked very well for the WEP and the engineering library. More important, it has worked for the students, who are directed to the right place to get help.

The last outreach component is the Women in Engineering Program orientation, which takes place before the start of the fall semester. It allows first-year women engineering students to learn about the Penn State engineering program, to work on engineering design team projects, and to meet other engineering students like themselves. The orientation fosters a sense of community in which students can easily mingle with the director of the WEP and the engineering faculty.

During the orientation, the students are introduced to the engineering reference librarian. The librarian takes them on a tour of the engineering library and helps them with their engineering design project assignments that are due before the end of the orientation. This setting creates the opportunity for the library contact to get to know the students and answer any questions they have about Penn State or the library. It also allows the students to see that the engineering library is a friendly, useful place and encourages them early on to identify the engineering reference librarian as someone who is interested in helping them as they progress through the academic program.

Collection Development: The Women in Engineering Collection

A major effort of the collaboration with the WEP is the development of the Penn State Women in Engineering Collection. It is the belief of those in the WEP and the engineering library that a significant need exists for women engineering students to be able to access materials on women engineers. With women making up only nine percent of the engineering workforce and three percent of the national academic faculty, the students rarely, if ever, hear about the accomplishments of such women and seldom view them as role models (Taylor 1997). This lack of visibility does nothing to encourage women students to stay in engineering. The library's collection of materials on women engineers is designed to stimulate students' interest in those women to learn more about them.

> The Penn State Women in Engineering Collection
> http://www.libraries.psu.edu/crsweb/eng/wie/
> Features a searchable database of the collection and links to women in engineering research resources.

The effort to locate and purchase materials on women engineers has been a difficult activity due to the small body of published literature. Because of this, the scope of the collection has been expanded to include materials on women who either are scientists, inventors, or industrial designers or are in other related occupations. This broad range also better reflects the diverse careers that women with engineering degrees often pursue.

In addition to biographies, the engineering library also collects workplace testimonials, statistical information, and government reports, because students often have other interests in women engineers beyond biographical information. Both traditional and nontraditional sources are used to develop the collection, including trade catalogs such as the *British National Bibliography*, society newsletters from groups such as the Women in Engineering Program Advocates Network (WEPAN), journals such as *SWE* (*Society of Women Engineers*), and Web sites such as the ADA Project Bibliographies.

Developing a Women in Engineering Collection: Where to Find Materials

• Start with the Penn State Women in Engineering Collection to get an idea of what types of resources are available in the subject area and who is publishing them. www.libraries.psu.edu/crsweb/eng/wie

• Look around at other women in science and engineering research Web sites to get more ideas. One good one is: Women in Science: A Guide to Reference Sources at Louisiana State University. http://www.lib.lsu.edu/sci/chem/guides/srs117.html

• Try women's studies research guides. They often feature bibliographies that cover women in science and engineering. A good example is the University of Wisconsin Women's Studies Librarian's Office Publications and Services. http://www.library.wisc.edu/libraries/WomensStudies/homemore.htm

• Periodically review the sites of the major women in science and engineering organizations, such as: Women in Engineering Program Advocates Network (WEPAN). http://www.wepan.org and the Society of Women Engineers (SWE) http://www.swe.org Both groups publish valuable reports, conference proceedings and other information on timely topics relevant to women in engineering.

• Search the web for women in engineering/science bibliographies. These are often full of great information. One good resource is the ADA Project Bibliographies http://ww.cs.yale.edu/homes/tap/tap-biblio.html

• Government publications are also a good source, especially for statistical information.

• The National Science Foundation produces some excellent materials http://www.nsf.gov

• Engineering and science education associations are another great resource. Try the American Society for Engineering Education. http://www.asee.org

• Among the many divisions of ASEE is Women in Engineering. The ASEE journal, ASEE Prism, frequently features articles on women in engineering and science as well as the annual conference proceedings.

• Check larger publication catalogs such at the British National Bibliography, which often has listings of women in science and women in engineering materials.

To better showcase the materials, the Penn State Women in Engineering Collection Web site has been created that includes a database of more than 250 materials on women in engineering, women in science and women inventors that are located in the engineering library and in other Penn State libraries. In addition to the database, the Web site features a link to the Penn State WEP Web site, links to other women in engineering and science collections and bibliographies, and links to a contact page to send comments and questions to the engineering library.

To further advertise the collection, book jackets of some of the materials and an informational flyer are put on display in an exhibit case located outside the engineering library, a heavily traveled area of one of the main engineering classroom buildings. The exhibit attracts a lot of attention. It is not uncommon to see students—men and women alike—looking at the exhibit. This has been a rather simple, but effective, way to call more attention to the collection.

Special Project: Enigmatic Computers

The last component of the collaboration, and perhaps the most interesting, is the enigmatic computers course. The course was created by the WEP in response to the lack of confidence that many women engineering students have in using computers. This lack of confidence is quite problematic for engineering students because much of the course work and many of the projects rely heavily on the use of computers. For some women, this may be a contributing factor in their decision to leave engineering.

Thus, the WEP, with help from the engineering reference librarian, created a basic, hands-on computer course for first-year women engineering students who believe they need to further develop their computing skills. Through the course, the students learn about basic computer hardware and become familiar with the software programs they need to know as Penn State students. The software programs taught are not purely engineering (such as C and AutoCAD). Instead, the course focuses on the general programs typically encountered in their early engineering classes (figure 1).

Enigmatic computers is taught by the WEP and the engineering reference librarian, and features women guest instructors from the College of Engineering as well as classroom assistants who are upper-level women engineering students. The course focuses less on grading the students' work and more on creating a positive learning environment. The goal is for the students to feel comfortable enough to ask questions, experiment with computers, and feel confident in themselves. In addition, they meet other women engineering students, the director of the WEP, and the engineering reference librarian, thus developing a support system they can rely on as they progress through the engineering program.

Although there is no library skills component to this course (students typically have library instruction sessions a few times in their first year), a

---

Figure 1
Enigmatic Computers Course Syllabus

Introduction to the computer lab
Computer hardware
Silverscreen software: Modeling and design
PowerPoint software: Presentations
EXCEL software: Spreadsheets
Internet and searching the Web
Research on the Web
Web page design
Basic HTML
Advanced HTML
Web page project: The life and work of a woman engineer

---

special Web page project provides the opportunity to teach research. For the project, students must select a woman engineer, scientist, or inventor; research her background and work accomplishments; and create a Web page to share with the class. To do this, the students are taught how to do research on the Web, to evaluate Web sites, and search the Women in Engineering Collection and use the Engineering Library to find books with biographical information. It is hoped that in addition to learning research skills, the exposure to and use of the Women in Engineering Collection will encourage the students to return to it throughout their time at Penn State, for personal study as well as class projects.

Summary
Through outreach, the development of the Women in Engineering Collection, and involvement in other projects, Penn State's engineering library has been an active participant in a supportive network committed to the success of women engineering students. Although it is difficult in this early stage to determine if these activities cause women engineering students to stay in the program, certainly the combined effort of the Engineering Library and the WEP creates a sense of community in which students feel encouraged and supported. With this encouragement and support from others, women students might be more likely to continue in the program and feel that they are not one of a few women in engineering but, rather, a member of the next generation of successful engineers.

References

Astin, Alexander W. 1993. Engineering outcomes. *ASEE PRISM* 3: 27-30.
Engineering Workforce Commission. 1997. *The 1996 Engineering and Technology Enrollments*. New York: American Association of Engineering Societies.

Lazarus, Barbara and Indira Nair. 1996. Bridging the gender gap in engineering and science: The case of institutional transformation. *Women in Engineering Conference: Capitalizing on Today's Challenges.* Women in Engineering Program Advocates Network.

Takahira, Sayrui, Goodings, Deborah J., and James P. Byrnes. 1998. Retention and performance of male and female engineering students: An examination of academic and environmental variables. *Journal of Engineering Education* 87: 297-304.

Taylor, Jenifer A. 1997. Warming a chilly classroom," *ASEE PRISM* 6: 29-33.

A Sampling of Published Accounts on Academic Library Diversity Activities

Greenfield, Louise W., Rawan, Atifa R. and Camille L. O' Neill. The diversity research guide program: The University of Arizona Library's experience. In *Multicultural Acquisitions.* Binghamton, NY: Haworth Press, 1993: 115-29.

Holmes, Barbara, and Arthur A. Lichtenstein. 1998. Minority student success: Librarians as partners. *College and Research Libraries News* 59:496-98.

Osborne, Nancy Seale, and Cecilia Poon. 1995. Serving diverse library populations through the specialized instructional services concept," *Reference Librarian* 51-52:285-94.

Stoffle, Carla J. 1990. A new library for the new undergraduate. *Library Journal* 115:47-50.

Suggested Readings on Women in Engineering

Baum, Eleanor. Recruiting and graduating women: The underrepresented student. 1990. *IEEE Communications Magazine* 28:47-50.

National Science Foundation. *Women and Minorities in Science and Engineering.* 1996. Arlington, Va: National Science Foundation.

Taylor, Jenifer A. 1997. Warming a chilly classroom. *ASEE PRISM* 6:29-33.

Women in Engineering Program Advocates Network. *Conference Proceedings from 1991- 1998.*

Penn State Women in Engineering Collection Web site: http://www.libraries.psu.edu/crsweb/eng/wie/

Information Literacy (LIB 150) at Fort Lewis College:
Innovative Approaches to Instruction in a Required Course

Tina Evans

> Access to and critical use of information and information technol-
> ogy is absolutely vital to lifelong learning, and accordingly no gradu-
> ate – indeed no person – can be judged educated unless he or she is
> 'information literate' and, to an extent, computer literate as well
> (Orr, Appleton, and Andrews 1996, 226).

Introduction
At this time, perhaps more than at any other, college and university faculty
and administrators are recognizing the critical need to help students become lifelong learners so that they can thrive in the rapidly changing information economy. Academic librarians are in a unique position to educate
students and campus communities in how to pursue learning through independent inquiry, critical evaluation, and use of information resources.
The information literacy course (LIB 150) taught at Fort Lewis College is
an integral component of the curriculum, and it serves as one model for
creatively integrating information skills and concepts into the educational
program.[1]

LIB 150 is one among several similar courses taught in academic libraries in the United States. It shares some philosophies and approaches with
those courses and with other library instruction programs, but it also demonstrates unique features that offer new models to the practice of library
instruction. These features include: (1) a theme-based orientation for the
course; (2) a comprehensive, Web-based coursepack; and (3) a unique approach to combining self-study and in-class activities. This chapter draws
connections among LIB 150 and other, similar library instruction efforts
and discusses the unique and innovative features of information literacy at
Fort Lewis College and how and why they were developed. Other points to
be explored include challenges, both past and future, of administering the
information literacy program.[2]

Program Overview
Fort Lewis College (FLC) is a four-year public liberal arts college in Durango,
Colorado, with a typical enrollment of approximately 4,300 students. LIB
150 is a one-credit course required for graduation. Students who enroll in
LIB 150 must have completed twelve units of college credit and must reg-

ister concurrently with Composition 150, the college's introductory composition course. During each fall and spring term, the library offers approximately ten sections of LIB 150, each with enrollment capped at forty. Typically, 350 to 400 freshman- and sophomore-level students register for the course each term. Several full-time and adjunct library professors teach one to two sections per term. The course is taught in an electronic classroom within the library. This room is equipped with twenty student computers, one instructor computer, two overhead computer/video projection units, and a sound system. The library instruction coordinator oversees course development, solicits input from other LIB 150 professors in developing the course, develops the class schedule for each term, provides teacher training and support (as necessary), participates in evaluating teaching performance of adjunct professors, develops most of the course content, and creates course management tools (such as grading spreadsheets).

Related Programs

A forum held at "Taking Learning Seriously," the American Association of Higher Education (AAHE) national conference held in March 1998, brought together twenty provosts from community, state, and private colleges as well as state and Research I universities. At this forum, one "item addressed was the importance of collaboration between librarians and university faculty and improved learning through these efforts" (Jenkins, Simoneaux, and Miller 1998). Librarians have traditionally offered "one-shot" bibliographic instruction sessions to classes at the request of individual faculty members. Such sessions are typically geared toward helping students complete research assignments in a given field of study or, even more specifically, for a given course. As the sheer volume of information rapidly expands, an increasing number of librarians, libraries, educational programs, entire schools, and various consortia are developing courses and programs designed to teach information literacy: the root concepts and skills required for one to pursue continual, independent, research-based learning.

The important collaborative work discussed by the provosts and librarians at the AAHE forum can take many forms. One form is the required, for-credit information literacy course developed and taught by library faculty. A major advantage of such a course is that it will likely reach all or nearly all students. It may not appear obvious how courses developed and taught through the library could involve collaboration with other teaching faculty, but by becoming and remaining in touch with the curriculum and by communicating with the faculty regarding expectations for student research and writing and regarding the changing nature of library research, librarians can create information literacy courses that complement the overall educational programs of their institutions. Because we librarians are typically the ones who most clearly understand the nature and importance of information literacy, we have something of high value to *add* to the curriculum, something best crafted by us and perhaps less likely to make its way into the curriculum via other channels. Effective, dynamic, required courses in information literacy represent a highly visible, integral means of accomplishing the kind of collaboration called for at the AAHE forum.

Individuals, institutions, and consortia in higher education are teaching information literacy using a variety of creative approaches. Some of those approaches include the use of Web-based instructional materials. Although LIB 150 at FLC is unique in a number of ways, it shares some characteristics with other instruction initiatives. This section highlights some of those programs and provides useful examples for instructors developing and teaching information literacy programs. Similarities and differences between the instruction efforts described here and FLC's LIB 150 are addressed later in this chapter.

The University of Arizona's Library Skills Program

UA's library skills program was an early effort to make learning a basic set of library research skills a required component of the undergraduate curriculum. Under this program, all students enrolled in English 101 were required to complete exercises from a library skills workbook in order to receive credit for the English class (a required course).

> The workbook introduced students to the physical layout of the building; reading call numbers; the reference area; finding background information; the catalog; periodicals and periodical indexes; newspapers; and the research process. The final assignment, called the search strategy, was designed for students to use to gather information for their research paper.... In its heyday the LSP was administered by a full time Library Skills Librarian. Approximately 260 introductory sessions a year were given to approximately 5500 students. In addition, the program employed 25 student assistants to staff an LSP desk in the reference area, to give presentations and to grade workbook assignments. Library staff were also asked to volunteer to give presentations.... By the early 1990s, at the request of the English Department, the LSP workbook assignments were no longer required for English 101. Library support for the program had diminished to the point that the LSP Librarian was a half time temporary position. There was no longer a separate reference desk for LSP questions and the program only employed 4 students to grade assignments (Library Skills Programs at U of A 1996).

The library skills program was an ambitious effort in library instruction. It focused on developing particular skills rather than on teaching research concepts, which was typical of the programs developed at that time. Perhaps in response to the rapidly changing nature of research and the rapid development of new research tools, current library instruction practice has shifted toward teaching conceptual material, de-emphasizing the development of specific skills. Following current trends and making use of the creative and interactive possibilities for instruction in the online environment, the University of Arizona is currently pursuing alternative methods of teaching information literacy, including encouraging the use of a new online tutorial, Research Instruction Online or RIO, available via the Web beginning in fall 1998 (Bender and Rosen 1998).[3]

Library Media Education (LME) 101 at Western Kentucky University

Another early and ambitious required course was developed at Western Kentucky University (WKU). According to program coordinator Linda Alexander, "For more than 30 years, WKU has required all freshmen and transfer students to take a one credit-hour course called Library Media Education (LME 101). The course seeks to introduce basic research strategies and information technology to approximately 2,400 students each year" (1995, 245–46). The program is taught by "one full-time coordinator and six graduate-student teaching assistants." As in UA's library skills program, the university prints its own text; course materials and presentations are fairly uniform across the sections.

> The course evolves around the completion of a bibliography which students prepare in segments and submit as their final assignment. Students select their own research topic, usually one that has been assigned in another course. Students use worksheets as aids in collecting sources for their bibliographies. They learn to locate books, periodicals, microforms, reference sources, and government documents by means of WKU's OPAC…, periodical and newspaper indexes, and GPO on SilverPlatter (Alexander 1995, 246–47).

The WKU program is ambitious in its content coverage and in the number of students it reaches. Although instruction in specific skills is probably occurring by means of research worksheets, Alexander's description implies that active learning and critical thinking are also emphasized through bibliography development.[4]

State University of New York (SUNY) Plattsburgh's LIB 101

The introduction to library research (LIB 101) program at SUNY Plattsburgh is another required, one-credit course; it has been part of the school's general education program since 1979. Carla List (1995, 385–86), coordinator of library education services, noted that approximately twenty-four sections averaging about thirty students each (about 720 students total) were being taught each semester. List comments that the program has been "moving away from a skills- and tools-based approach to a concept-based approach," a move typical of recent innovations in library instruction.

At SUNY Plattsburgh, the program began with a unified curriculum and has evolved to include a number of sections that focus on broad disciplinary areas, such as the social sciences. These sections are geared toward students majoring in these areas. Various versions of the course have been developed and taught to students who self-select a course section with a broad disciplinary emphasis. General sections have been continued as well (List 1995, 391–94). Although there are some obvious benefits to specialization, including the ability to teach more specific material related to a student's chosen area of study, List notes some drawbacks to the disciplinary approach: (1) the tendency for instruction to become more tool oriented as the disciplinary focus narrows; (2) the labor-intensiveness of teaching multiple versions of the LIB 101 course; (3) focus problems within such broad disciplinary groupings; (4) complications in administering the course; and (5) students registering for time slots instead of subjects and thereby registering for inappropriate sections (List 1995, 395–97). Perhaps the advantages of specialization outweigh the drawbacks at SUNY Plattsburgh, however. The spring 1998 schedule available online showed twenty-one specialized sections of LIB 101 and no general sections (Division of Library and Information Services Instruction Group 1998).

Information Research Course at Cabrillo College
This one-credit, self-paced course offered at a two-year college addresses a wide range of information literacy goals.

Students enrolled in Information Research — Library 10 will become familiar with the organization of a library and the different types of access tools available, including computerized databases. They will learn to recognize the different levels, types, and formats of information and their appropriate uses. The student will be introduced to the conventions of scholarly research, such as proper citation, and intellectual property rights. Upon completion of this course the student will have learned how to construct a research strategy, as well as evaluate the information gathered for its content, source, quality and relevance (Jones 1996).

Course objectives described on the library's Web site emphasize that students will learn to locate and evaluate information available in a broad variety of formats and locations, both inside and outside libraries. Such sources include printed books and periodicals, online media, and oral information. For ten years, Information Research has been a corequisite to Cabrillo's English 1A composition course. About 800 to 1,000 students take the course each semester (Smalley 1998).

As with several other programs discussed in this chapter, the librarians at the Robert E. Swenson Library publish their own workbook. A fairly lengthy excerpt from these materials is available for viewing from the library Web site (Jones 1996). The example provided demonstrates a highly personalized, informal tone; at the same time, it challenges students to think independently and critically. The materials appear to cover research concepts clearly and somewhat in depth; such coverage is essential in materials intended for independent study. Information Research is a fairly comprehensive, introductory-level information literacy course.

The Internet Navigator Project in Utah

Internet Navigator is "Utah's first on-line, multi-institutional Internet course" (Internet Navigator 1996). Student information available on the course Web site describes the course administration:

> The Internet Navigator is a self paced, independent study course. Students taking the course will be expected to take responsibility for their own schedule and their own learning. A preceptor is available to every student. At least one preceptor is located at every college or university currently offering the course in Utah. The preceptor will grade students' work and help students with any questions they may have (Internet Navigator 1998).

All course materials are available online. Students conduct Internet research, develop their own evaluation criteria for Internet sources, and evaluate sources based on those criteria. These activities parallel activities conducted in several other courses described here; however, the scope of research materials used in the Navigator course is narrowed solely to the online environment. Students do gain experience with some valuable types of resources (e-mail discussion lists and newsgroups) that, based on the examples gathered here, seem to be taught infrequently in research courses. Internet searching instruction is probably more in depth in this course than it is in courses attempting to cover a wider variety of information sources (Internet Navigator 1998).

Purdue Libraries Undergraduate Tutorial Online (PLUTO)

> PLUTO was begun in the spring of 1995 by a team of Purdue Librarians and computing professionals. Its primary purpose is to meet the goals for orientation level instruction and motivate students to learn more about finding and using information effectively through a learner centered, self-paced approach. Purdue Libraries administration supported the development of PLUTO through equipment and programming funds. PLUTO is an ongoing project under constant revision. The project has been "beta" tested on over 400 students (About the PLUTO Project 1995).

PLUTO is designed to improve students' database-searching abilities. Instruction focuses on keyword searching because this searching method is both highly flexible and difficult to master. PLUTO is divided into three areas: "searching by keyword," "Using THOR, The Online Resource" (which includes the Purdue online catalog, other library catalogs, and several periodicals indexes), and "Locating THOR Material" (physically accessing materials identified through THOR) (PLUTO 1995).

PLUTO is an ambitious, innovative project geared toward providing basic research instruction via the Internet. Begun in 1995, it represents an early effort to use the Web for library instruction. Like the Internet Navigator course, all materials are online, including quizzes on concepts and skills taught. PLUTO teaches both concept-oriented material and detailed, procedural information related to conducting research at Purdue. This dual approach (combining instruction in general concepts with enough detail specific to the given school's library to allow students to gain a foothold in conducting independent research) is popular in current library instruction programs.

PLUTO also contains online record-keeping functions that allow teaching faculty to assign the tutorial in their courses and receive notification of each student's quiz score (PLUTO quiz introduction 1995). This type of online record-keeping can be a real time-saver for those administering and teaching online courses in any subject area, and such features will be ever more important to those of us teaching large numbers of students in the online environment.

Capital Community-Technical College Library and Information Skills Workbook

The online Capital Community-Technical College Library and Information Skills Workbook presents a self-paced, fairly comprehensive, introductory-level information literacy tutorial. The online introduction outlines the goals of the tutorial:

"This tutorial is designed to achieve the following goals:
- To teach you the basics of library and information research; and
- To teach you how to use Capital Community College Library.

After you have read each chapter of the tutorial and completed the assignments, you should be able to:
- Find a book using the computerized catalog and locate it on the shelf;
- Use the computerized catalog to determine whether a book has been checked out;
- Use journal and newspaper indexes to locate current information on specific subjects;
- Evaluate sources of information for author bias and authority;
- Learn to develop a search strategy.

The goal of the tutorial is to make you feel comfortable and confident while doing library research" (DeLoatch and O'Connor 2000).

This workbook covers a great deal of ground in teaching information literacy, including using books, periodicals, and Internet sources for research and evaluating individual sources available in these formats. It also teaches some skills specific to using the Capital Community-Technical College Library and thus offers a mix of conceptual and skill-oriented instruction.

Like PLUTO, the workbook includes periodic online quizzes on material covered intended to help students gauge their learning progress. But the workbook demonstrates yet another online innovation: It includes an online evaluation form to be filled out by those who complete the tutorial. The evaluation form is not anonymous, however; the content of signed evaluations may vary considerably from those submitted anonymously. Still, this form is an excellent way to solicit input from the workbook's users.

The LIB 150 Program

Information literacy at Fort Lewis College is probably most similar in scope and depth to the credit courses offered at Western Kentucky University, Cabrillo College, and SUNY Plattsburgh, the main difference being the format in which our course is offered. In this respect, the FLC course more closely resembles the Internet Navigator course, PLUTO, and the Capital Community-Technical College Library and Information Skills Workbook tutorial, all of which are offered in the online environment. This section explains the origins of the LIB 150 program and describes its science fiction theme, learning objectives, teaching methodology, and general course assessment results.

Writing Program Reform

Stamatoplos and Mackoy (1998) note that college students need library instruction and that mere exposure to a library does not usually help them learn good research skills. In their review of the library instruction literature, they also note that "instructed students used a wider variety of sources, made greater use of catalogs, and showed more use of various libraries and services.... Instruction produced significant improvements in students' tested library knowledge and use" (324–25). A study by Daragan and Stevens (1996, 75) used pre- and posttest measures to demonstrate increased levels of student information literacy after library instruction. They also note that library instruction levels the playing field by encouraging students to develop a base level of research knowledge and skills, thereby effectively decreasing variance in information literacy skills demonstrated among students.

Fortunately, during the most recent writing program reform at FLC, the faculty articulated a desire for students to begin learning research concepts and skills early in their college careers. The old writing program included research-based writing activities. The new program focused on developing students' scholarly reading and thinking abilities by having them read and analyze a given set of texts. Writing activities were no longer research based. At the time of the reform (1994 and 1995), many faculty members saw this new model as an effective means of developing scholarly habits of mind in freshman- and sophomore-level college students, but many also lamented losing the research component of the old program. Thus, the library faculty were invited to develop and teach a new required course: information literacy. Librarians welcomed this invitation to participate so visibly in the educational program.

To help the library faculty meet these new responsibilities, the administration funded the addition of one new library faculty member. This addition was very helpful, but it did not provide enough support to fully cover the increase in activity resulting from developing and teaching a required class. The challenge was deemed well worth it, however, for the sake of integrating library instruction into the curriculum. Managing the load placed on librarians has been a focus of administering and managing the program since its inception. Efforts to effectively handle the increased demands of offering the information literacy course are discussed below.

The Theme

Like the WKU program described above, LIB 150 is "standardized to expose all students to the same basic competencies" (Alexander 1995, 249) and is required for graduation. Like our counterparts at WKU, we librarians at FLC have found that because our course is required, students have increased incentives to do well in it. On the other hand, we have also found that some students resent being forced to take any course and the fact that LIB 150 is required can cause students to have a bad impression of it even before attending the first class. Overcoming this sentiment is our first challenge in the classroom, and the theme orientation of the class described here is, in part, an attempt to surprise students on the first day, upset their preconceptions about the course, and thereby make them more receptive to the course in general.

Because research for LIB 150 is not linked to writing a paper for another course, as the library instruction coordinator, I felt that without some context, some information need (real or simulated), students would feel that the course was without meaning. Elayne Walstedter, outreach librarian at FLC, mentioned using role-playing in instruction activities. The idea of role-playing intrigued me, and I began looking for a unifying theme for LIB 150 that would allow students to assume meaningful roles as researchers—roles they could maintain throughout the course.

I wanted the theme to be something truly out of the ordinary—something that would surprise students and, possibly, begin to dispel any unfavorable preconceptions they might bring to this newly required library course. I also thought a video introduction might intrigue students and make the theme more tangible. With these outcomes in mind, I began looking for a science fiction theme that would work, preferably a story that had been made into a film. I used several reference works on science fiction in my search. The *Encyclopedia of Science Fiction* (Clute and Nicholls 1993, 382–84) was most helpful because it contained review articles on common genre themes. The near-apocalypse theme seemed particularly useful for role-playing; a story with such a theme would offer a wide range of roles that could be assumed, and the seriousness of the situation might encourage the students to engage in thoughtful introspection when choosing their roles.

The entry in the *Encyclopedia of Science Fiction* on the book and film *When Worlds Collide* (1951) particularly intrigued me. When I watched the film, it seemed perfect for providing our unifying theme for LIB 150. In the movie, two heavenly bodies are hurtling toward Earth. The first of them narrowly misses our planet but causes a great deal of destruction because of its gravitational pull. The second asteroid directly impacts Earth and destroys it. Only forty or fifty people survive this disaster. They build a rocket ship to fly to the first heavenly body—a habitable planet—passing by Earth. At the end of the movie, the survivors open their ship door and gaze out on a lush new planet where they will build their new society.

Students in LIB 150 view key scenes from the movie and then assume the roles of the survivors by deciding what role they will play in the new planet's society. Their research assignments help prepare them to fulfill their roles. A Personal Interest and Experience Questionnaire (T. Greenwood 1998c) and a Topic Selection Advice Sheet (T. Greenwood 1998d) in the LIB 150 coursepack encourage students to choose topics meaningful to them by helping them explore their talents and values.

Role-playing brings some valuable side benefits to our library instruction course. Students are encouraged to make something resembling a career choice within the context of contributing to society in a way they find personally meaningful because it is based on their own talents and values. This exercise is a wonderful practice run for the important educational and career choices that undergraduate students must make. This role-playing also helps students understand the why behind information literacy; it helps them see how research and learning can be vehicles for personal growth and can help one respond to various situations.

Learning Objectives and Teaching Methodology

The SUNY Plattsburgh course ties library instruction to a disciplinary focus, an effective way to make library instruction meaningful to students who choose their focus well. List noted some problems with this approach, however: "the focused sections may become much more tool-oriented than the generic sections"; the program became more labor-intensive for librarians due to developing and teaching multiple versions; and "some students still register for a time slot rather than a subject interest" (1995, 395–97).

Our course at FLC is standardized and contains no disciplinary focus. The need to streamline the labor-intensiveness of the course is one of the reasons for choosing this model, but not the only reason. At SUNY Plattsburgh, teaching and learning about communication cycles within a disciplinary setting can readily occur in the focused sections of LIB 101 (List 1995, 390). Understanding these cycles can greatly improve a student's ability to research and write in his or her chosen field. Because the FLC course is general, we devote little if any time to such specifics, but we have multiple opportunities to compare overall communication styles and purposes in various disciplines. These comparisons help students understand why professional communications take various forms. They begin to understand the considerations of practicality, timeliness, and prestige that drive scholarly and other publication choices. We target our program to help students develop a base level of skills and concepts applicable to research activities in various disciplines. We also encourage them to recognize some of the differences among disciplines with regard to research and publication and to understand that these differences result from the communication needs of those active in the discipline and not from mere chance.

By placing no real constraints on topic choice other than societal contribution, we provide LIB 150 students with the unique educational experience of conducting free and open inquiry, an experience that can serve as a model for their future information use whether it be within or outside their academic career. Some students have used this opportunity to explore occupational topics they may not be able to explore in other classes. One of my students chose to play the role of a police officer. By the end of the course, he was seriously considering becoming one! In his final exam essay, he wrote with enthusiasm about pursuing this career path and mentioned he would soon be going on a "ride-along" with a local law enforcement officer. When students use LIB 150 research opportunities well, they can have a powerful experience. At the very least, they have an opportunity to experiment with life choices and to use information to support them.

We pursue an approach to teaching information literacy that coincides with the approach described by Vishwanatham, Wilkins, and Jevec (1997, 438): "the underlying principle [is] that the course materials should serve as a starting point from which users ... gain the skills to teach themselves and remain up to date with the applications relevant to their needs." This approach mirrors the "trend in library education away from tool-based instruction and toward concept-based instruction" described by Ercegovac (1995, 250), among others. However, as evidenced in the programs described above, library educators still recognize the need to provide students with enough specifics to allow them to use certain sets of tools available at their institutions and/or via the Internet. This instruction is most often combined with teaching concepts that enable students to pursue the kind of independent learning and adapting described above. The FLC course pursues this dual objective by providing instruction in specifics such as Netscape and e-mail software use, library catalog search conventions, and general periodicals index use, combined with generalized material about Boolean search techniques, truncation in database searching, controlled vocabularies, source evaluations, and more. Students use the conceptual and skill-based information we have provided when they complete research activities to fulfill their information needs as they assume new societal roles. Using this approach, we hope to give students a foothold where conducting independent research is concerned, but we also hope the foundational concepts learned in LIB 150 will allow students to teach themselves new research tools and strategies in the future.

In our approach to teaching information literacy, we librarians at FLC agree wholeheartedly with the following statement made by Orr, Appleton, and Andrews:

> Access to, and critical use of information and of information technology is absolutely vital to lifelong learning, and accordingly no graduate—indeed no person—can be judged educated unless he or she is 'information literate' and, to an extent, computer literate as well (1996, 226).

Because "the modern work world often requires employees to communicate electronically and to work on projects with others at distant locations" (Dewald 1996b, 173), we incorporate the use of communication technologies such as e-mail as required components of our course. Student topic selections must be e-mailed to professors. Professors respond to these choices and notify students of their assignment grades via e-mail only. Students must access and read their e-mail to discover whether their choices are acceptable and to get their grades for each assignment. Beginning in fall 1998, students have also been required to sign up for an e-mail discussion list created for their professor and classmates, an activity that introduces them to this means of communicating now vital in many professions. Students also learn basic Web use and searching. In fact, the coursepack is available via the Web only.

Because valuable information is currently published in such a wide variety of media, LIB 150 assignments center on locating information in selected formats. The first research assignment asks students to locate topical material published in books, the second requires use of periodicals, and the third requires students to locate nonprint materials, defined as Internet-based information, films, videos, sound recordings, oral information, and more (T. Greenwood 1998b). For each assignment, students must locate resources available in the format(s) specified by the assignment, write complete citations in MLA style for the materials they find, and compose evaluative paragraphs for each listed resource. Criteria are provided to help students evaluate the information they find (T. Greenwood 1999b; Greenwood and Frisbie 1999; T. Greenwood 1998b). In our course, the importance of traditional publications, such as printed books and journals, is stressed, but we recognize the growing importance of electronic publications. We agree with the following statement made by Malone and Videon:

> The authors project greater use of electronic resources in the near future as more full text serial databases become available and user friendly. Our findings in this study suggest that adequate instruction is needed to help students overcome the technological and intellectual barriers to access and to give them clear patterns for citing electronic resources (1997, 158).

Malone and Videon also observe that:

> Faculty members themselves have generally not used electronic resources long enough to feel completely comfortable with the citation format, and there seems to be some question as to who is responsible for this type of instruction (157).

Because clear citations are a vital component of the scholarly communication process and thus are integral to the research process itself, we FLC librarians decided we are responsible for teaching proper citation format in our research course. We hope students who have completed LIB 150 will demonstrate more uniform ways of citing online resources than students did prior to the inception of the course. Perhaps when students demonstrate clear, understandable citations, the comfort level for using online sources on campus will increase.

After students have located and evaluated resources in all the required formats, they complete a final bibliography project, which calls on them to evaluate and synthesize their findings as well as to reflect on the research strategies they used. Students must choose, from among their ten sources, the five that would be most useful in performing their new societal role. Each student must then write a one- to three-paragraph essay justifying the choices made (T. Greenwood 2000). This final bibliography and writing exercise allows students to make comparisons across formats and to assess not only content value, but also the value of the format of presentation itself as related to a given information use. Finally, the students write a second one- to three-paragraph essay describing their search strategies and identifying how their strategies evolved throughout the class. Students are especially encouraged to identify how they would improve their strategies for future research endeavors. This reflection on a completed research process brings closure to the course in a way that identifies LIB 150 course content as a base upon which students will be expected to build as they progress through college.[5]

Assessment Results

At FLC, we have used three assessment instruments for our information literacy course: a pretest/posttest, a self-evaluative "final exam" essay, and an anonymous online student course evaluation. The pretest/posttest is currently in use as is the online student course evaluation. Many elements of the self-evaluative essay have been incorporated into the final bibliography project described above.

The pretest/posttest was implemented in the spring trimester of 1997, and the third version of the test is currently in use. It is a multiple-choice test covering skill-based and conceptual course content. Students who perform well enough on the pretest are allowed to have the LIB 150 course requirement waived, so there are clear incentives to take the test seriously. Unfortunately, originally there were no such incentives for the posttest, which was not used in the grading process. Still, students demonstrated noticeable, if not dramatic, improvements in their knowledge and skills on the posttest. During the 1999–2000 academic year, LIB 150 professors encouraged students to review course material prior to taking the posttest by awarding individual students extra credit points for significant improvement.

The first version of the pretest/posttest was used for three trimesters. During this time, the course format and content changed considerably. The test provided a basis for comparing student learning in the new self-study version of the course (described below) with that of the old lecture-based format.

The self-evaluative final exam essay was composed of the following questions:

• What about this class, or something you learned in this class, surprised you, and how?

• How have your notions about library research changed or stayed the same?

• How would you feel if you were assigned a big research project today? Would you feel well prepared? Would you feel confused or lost as to where to begin? Why? Would anything you learned from this class be helpful? If so, what?

• How did playing a role as a survivor of planetary disaster affect your learning in this class?

• (Optional) Are there any other comments you'd like to make (T. Greenwood 1998b)?

Students were much more positive than negative in their essays in assessing how much they learned and the value of that learning to their future research activities. A majority of students also seemed to feel that the theme orientation of the course was helpful to their learning. In their final evaluative essays, our students often ended up discussing the library in general and remarking how pleasantly surprised they were at the number of resources available to them at or through the library and how easy it was to access research materials. These statements sharply contrasted with students' statements concerning their feelings of fear and discomfort when they attempted to use the library for research prior to taking LIB 150. Many students were probably overestimating their research abilities after completing LIB 150, but this overconfidence is preferable to research anxiety. Stamatoplos and Mackoy (1998, 333) note that "increasing patrons' confidence in their skill at using libraries in itself has a positive impact on their perception of the library." These positive perceptions may encourage further research activity by students.

Of course, even though students were told they would not be graded down for making negative statements about the course, they more than likely felt some pressure to be positive in their assessments of the course and their performance in it because the final exam essay was a graded assignment. So, an anonymous course evaluation form was developed to solicit honest feedback from students regarding the course itself and the class professor through use of ratings and an open-ended comment section. This evaluation process has elicited some negative comments not present in the final exam essays. However, the overall character of these evaluations has remained consistent to a surprising degree with the character of the graded exams.

These three assessment instruments provide useful feedback about student academic achievement as well as student perceptions of the library and the course. The information gathered through these instruments is used in course development.

Course Management and Administration
Central Development of Coursepack, Syllabus, and Grading Policies

As was the case for several other library instruction programs discussed above, we at FLC developed and printed our own coursepack as the required text for LIB 150. For the LME 101 program at Western Kentucky University, Alexander (1995, 246) noted that new editions of their self-produced course materials were needed each year. We, too, soon realized a continual need for revision of course materials. The first edition of the coursepack was issued in fall 1996, and a second edition was produced and used in spring 1997. Avoiding wasting library resources by printing too many coursepacks for a given term required reasonably accurate estimates of the number of students who would purchase them. Still, a number of printed coursepacks went to waste with the first two editions. Teachers also noted that some students were using the outdated first edition in spring 1997.

These students probably obtained the first edition from friends who had already taken the course. This reusing of coursepacks further complicated both teaching the course and determining how many coursepacks to print for a given term. Using a Web-based coursepack eliminated these problems. Web-based course materials are discussed in detail below.

E-mailed "Tips"

As library instruction coordinator, I wanted to assist my colleagues, particularly new librarians and those who had never taught credit courses, with their regular preparation and teaching activities related to LIB 150. I decided that one of the best ways to help would be to teach the section of the course that fell earliest in the week so that I would always be the first to broach new subject material. Directly after my teaching of this section, I wrote informal "tips," which I e-mailed to all those teaching the course. These tips typically included details about how I approached teaching a given subject, including information such as the examples I used, materials I had prepared and made available to other teachers, effective concept explanations, and more. I discussed what worked well for me and warned others away from approaches I found to be less than optimal. As necessary, I also included administrative reminders for teachers. I encouraged others to write and e-mail their own tips, especially when they developed useful in-class activities or when they wanted to share a particularly effective way of presenting a concept. Although no other teachers offered tips of their own in the first term that LIB 150 was taught, they have shared some excellent ones since then. Teachers have appreciated the weekly tips, and I believe this regular communication encourages an atmosphere of sharing where classroom activities and materials are concerned. I encourage others to experiment with this type of communication among library educators when more than one librarian teaches a given subject or course.

Grading Help

Grading citation formats and evaluative paragraphs for all students in each section taught was an extremely time-intensive activity for professors. Furthermore, the thought of repeating this work at like intensity for the foreseeable future was not pleasing and I feared we would eventually suffer from burnout. However, we teachers agreed as a group that writing the citations and evaluations is an extremely valuable learning experience for students, an experience at the heart of the course itself and one that must be continued. So, I began to look for ways to decrease both the teaching and grading burdens on individual professors, particularly those who teach more than one section of LIB 150.

From my library director, I requested and obtained funding to hire student assistants for the course and began recruiting from among my best former students — students interested in the course and who performed at a very high level. Using this method, I have recruited some excellent student workers who have proved to be highly capable of problem-solving and working with minimal supervision. Each of these students has graded citation formats for teachers who have requested grading help, and one student has assisted with grading evaluative paragraphs using a content check off sheet (see figure 1). I also approached one librarian who does not teach the course about temporarily assisting with grading evaluative paragraphs, and he graciously agreed to help during the fall 1997 term.

Figure 1
LIB 150 Grading Sheet

_____ Narrowness of subject coverage
_____ Value as preparation for new societal role
_____ To be taken for future reference or read before trip
_____ Date published and effect on value of source
_____ Readability
_____ Organization of content
_____ Presence or absence of citations and effect on value of source
_____ Credibility of source (based on author, publisher, and/or other criteria)

Adjuncts

The fact that graduate teaching assistants are the only LME 101 teachers besides the program coordinator at WKU implies that other library instruction programs face similar problems with the labor-intensive nature of a required, for-credit course (Alexander 1995, 245). Alexander also notes that using graduate students as teachers is cost-effective and suggests that others should consider this model (248). Because FLC does not currently offer graduate programs, we do not have a readily available pool of graduate students who might be trained as teachers of the course. Nevertheless, my goal is to develop a pool of adjunct library professors interested in teaching one or two sections of the course per term so as to allow full-time librarians some flexibility where teaching is concerned. I approached my director with this idea, and she secured funding to hire one adjunct professor, a local medical librarian who had also recently worked reference part-time at our library. After an initial training period, this first adjunct professor taught one section of the course. She taught two in the fall of 1998, and I have secured support to continue hiring part-time professors to develop the adjunct teacher pool. The training for adjuncts has typically taken place as follows:

　　1.　For one term, newly hired adjuncts assist other teachers, primarily by grading the content of evaluative paragraphs, but also by assisting with grading citation formats. During this time, they also may oversee some of the grading done by student assistants and must observe key lectures/demonstrations given by other LIB 150 professors. They also receive all e-mailed tips and attend LIB 150 teacher meetings where course development and implementation are discussed.

2.   The following term, new adjuncts teach one section of the course, assist at the reference desk, and continue to receive all communications and attend all meetings (usually one or two per term) regarding the course. I sit in on class sessions if the adjunct professor requests it. Otherwise, the new adjuncts experiment with teaching the course and begin to develop their own style of teaching key concepts.

3.   The next term, adjuncts may teach two sections of LIB 150 and assist at the reference desk. They will continue to receive course-related communications and attend LIB 150 meetings. For evaluation purposes, the library director and I both view one class session of the adjunct professor's choice during this term and all subsequent terms in which the adjunct teaches.

4.   Adjuncts may continue to teach one to two sections per term as long as they receive satisfactory evaluations. They are expected to steadily improve as LIB 150 teachers, and they may contribute to the future development of the course.

Due to a necessary increase in LIB 150 sections and the loss of two adjunct professors who secured full-time employment, the library hired new adjunct professors for the fall of 2000 who did not have a chance to undergo the usual training. When hiring professionals for part-time work, an organization must expect a reasonable amount of turnover and be ready to improvise strategies to handle staffing crunches. Full-time librarians at Fort Lewis are considering a mentoring model for adjunct professors to assist these new teachers in the program. Having part-time teachers available to teach the course has allowed full-time FLC librarians some flexibility in deciding whether and how much they teach.

Self-study

As a one-credit course, LIB 150 classes originally met one hour per week throughout each school term.[6] During these sessions, individual professors lectured, conducted demonstrations, and led their students in hands-on activities. These sessions allowed teachers to reinforce concepts covered in the course readings, but much content not available in the coursepack was also covered. A number of students in each section found the in-class repetition of content covered in the readings frustrating, and it seemed quite possible that these students, given clear examples in the readings, would be capable of some independent learning regarding library research techniques and tools. This group of students resembled the "techies" described by Vishwanatham, Wilkins, and Jevec in their article on online instruction:

One group might be called "techies," or experts. Already familiar with the systems, techies tend to be impatient with formal instruction and prefer detailed descriptions or instruction sheets they can figure out for themselves. The other group might be considered "technologically challenged," as they consider themselves to be unfamiliar with either the system in use or computers in general. This group desires specific examples, detailed instruction, and the opportunity to try things out one step at a time with supportive coaching or counseling....Differences in skill levels and information needs are bound to limit the effectiveness of group instruction (1997, 434).

As was true at the inception of the course, several "technologically challenged" students are in each LIB 150 section. Though their numbers continue to decrease markedly, we cannot disregard this group's need for detailed, in-person instruction.[7] At the same time, we recognize that weekly class meetings have helped some students much more than others.

Furthermore, I predicted that an endless stream of weekly LIB 150 lectures, even given the foreseeable evolution of the course, might have a numbing effect on librarians who continued to teach the course long into the future. Diverse student needs, combined with these concerns for librarian job satisfaction, served as the impetus for developing a self-study version of LIB 150.

Six of ten LIB 150 sections offered in the fall of 1998 included self-study components. These sections met a handful of times over the course of the term, and much course content was conveyed via online materials. These materials are discussed in detail below. During the 1998–1999 academic year, several sections of the course were also offered in the old weekly meeting mode to accommodate those students who felt unprepared to handle the online format of the self-study materials and/or the responsibilities of keeping up with a class that rarely meets. Beginning in the fall of 1999, all sections of LIB 150 became self-study courses with individual professors offering additional, out-of-class assistance to students as necessary.[8] I agree with the creators of Utah's Internet Navigator online course who stated that Internet "delivery provides a valuable alternative to traditional library instruction. By incorporating new technologies to automate basic instruction, and focusing on student-centered approaches, libraries can instruct more users, accommodate more learning styles, and meet the needs of a more diverse clientele" (Hansen and Lombardo 1997, 76).

Note that this new delivery model for LIB 150 is self-study, not self-paced; many online courses offered in a variety of subject areas are self-paced. For our particular purposes, my colleagues and I agreed that a self-paced model would not be optimal for several reasons:

- Our students are typically freshman- and sophomore-level undergraduates who tend to be less independently motivated than the graduate students toward whom many online courses are targeted. The developers of the Internet Navigator course, also an introductory-level course, noted that "some students lacked the motivation or self-discipline to work successfully within the self-paced, independent environment, and might have benefited from more rigid deadlines and schedules" (Hansen and Lombardo 1997, 74). We feel many of our students would fall into this category should we follow a self-paced model.

• Our course is required for graduation, and we feel students would benefit by finishing it in a timely manner.

• Our course is introductory in nature, and students must complete it early in their academic program in order to reap the greatest benefit from what they have learned by building on the course's conceptual foundation as they continue to refine their research abilities. The possibilities of some students dragging the course out over several terms or years or of their turning in all their assignments at the end of the term are both decidedly unattractive to LIB 150 professors.

To help keep students on track under the self-study model, teachers enforce strict assignment deadlines and require periodic online quizzes on assigned course readings.

Summary Notes on Course Management and Administration

As demonstrated by our pretest/posttest results, students learn at least as much in the self-study mode and often more than they did under prior versions of our information literacy course.[9] Also, this new format frees up librarians to work in other capacities, which makes developing and maintaining self-study materials well worth the effort.

Web-based Course Materials
Why This Format?

As mentioned above, converting the print-based course materials to Web format eliminated the need to print entire new editions of the coursepack each term, or at least each year, in order to reflect current research practice. Furthermore, my colleagues and I believe that computer literacy and information literacy are inextricably intertwined, a belief shared by other librarians. The mission statement of the Division of Library and Information Services Instruction Program at SUNY Plattsburgh demonstrates this interrelationship between information literacy and computer literacy:

> In support of the Plattsburgh SUNY mission, the Division's Instruction Program enables all members of the College community to achieve information and computer literacy. Information literacy is defined as a group of critical thinking skills which consists of individuals' abilities to identify when they have an informational need and to use any necessary technology to access, evaluate, and

use information effectively. Computer literacy is defined as the understanding of what computers can and cannot do, and the ability to use both hardware and software appropriately and skillfully (Division of Library and Information Services 1997).

My own long-standing interest in using the Web for library services also made me keenly aware of possibilities for Web-based instruction. By early 1996, I had come to see the Web's potential as a unifying format through which materials could be brought together in new and creative ways that employ multimedia (T. Greenwood 1997, 66). I made the following statement in a chapter about my experiences coordinating the development of the original Western Illinois University Library Web site.

> Development of multimedia presentations that can actually teach users research skills and provision of direct access to "connected" information products in a wide variety of formats (as opposed to access to citations to printed material) will add to the library Web's value (T. Greenwood 1997, 74).

Using the Web to teach library research seemed especially appropriate at FLC because so many resources—our library catalog and those of other libraries, Internet-accessible databases to which our library subscribes, free Internet-accessible databases, a countless variety of Web-based information resources as well as many CD-ROM products to which we subscribe and which we launch via the Web—are available directly through our library Web site. In fact, the Reed Library Web is the central organizing point for accessing and/or learning about available information products and services (A. Greenwood 1997).

After two years of experience with the Web-based self-study version of the course, we at FLC can say with conviction what the creators of the Internet Navigator course in Utah said about their experience:

> This course also illustrates that Web-based instruction is not only feasible, but popular with traditional and nontraditional students. Moreover, it reinforces the need for students to take responsibility for their own learning (Hansen and Lombardo 1997, 75).

By combining uses of personal e-mail, LIB 150 section e-mail discussion lists, Web-based readings and quizzes, an online calendar for each class section, and occasional class meetings, we are now reaping the benefits described by Nancy Dewald of using computer-mediated communications in education:

> CMC [computer-mediated communication] can ... create a more egalitarian learning environment in which attention is no longer

focused on a teacher at the front of the classroom, and in which all participants can exercise initiative and control in discussion. CMC also allows learning to continue beyond the classroom by both increasing the availability of the instructor and providing access to outside resources (1996b, 170).

E-mail is particularly useful in our environment in which adjunct professors may be physically present in the library for very limited hours each week as it allows these professors to remain in contact with students. E-mail communication saves the time of both teacher and student because it is asynchronous, making lengthy games of phone tag unnecessary.

Asynchronicity is also a general characteristic of the Web-based instruction mode. "Asynchronicity has been found to increase the efficiency and flexibility of the classroom"[10] as well as the ease and flexibility of access (Dewald 1996a, 75). Presenting course materials on Web pages allows students to move around freely within the materials to access and review content, as needed, during the class and for future reference. The multimedia nature of the Web can also aid in reaching students with different learning styles.[11] I also hope that by using and becoming comfortable with Web-based course materials, students will more likely use online help as well as additional instructional materials available via the Reed Library Web.

Like other library educators (West and Ruess 1995, 140), in the not so distant past, I noted that many students in library instruction sessions and courses demonstrated little, if any, experience with electronic communication and information media. However, my colleagues and I continue to observe rapid changes in this area. Few students currently enrolling in LIB 150 sections have never used e-mail or the Web, in contrast with the fairly high number of students who fell into this category in the fall of 1996. The time is ripe for utilizing the Web for instruction, and because of their diminishing numbers, we will have time to personally assist those who most need our help in this new learning environment.

Further adding to the Web's appeal as a vehicle for instruction, Jayne and Vander Meer (1997, 133) suggest that "successful campus projects that showcase innovative pedagogy are effective in recruiting students and new faculty." Choosing the Web as the medium for the LIB 150 coursepack made sense for many reasons, and it provided my colleagues and me with the opportunity to teach in a new and innovative way.

Coursepack Content Development

The previous versions of the coursepack, both print and online, did not contain the full course content. Much of what was taught was presented in live lectures and demonstrations. In order to offer the course in a self-study mode, this lecture content had to be added to the existing coursepack. For self-study sections, occasional class meetings offer supplementary course content and allow students to seek help with difficult concepts and experiment with what they have learned by participating in hands-on activities. The information literacy coursepack on the Web contains the following:

- the syllabus;
- instructional Web pages containing textual material supplemented by graphical visual aids;
- all course assignments;
- streaming audio, virtual "lectures" with accompanying Web-based outline text;
- a teacher contact page providing information on how to reach each LIB 150 professor in person or by phone or e-mail and containing photographs of professors, some teacher self-introductions produced using streaming video, and some links to individual professors' personal Web pages;
- an online calendar system for accessing information specific to each section;
- an online quiz system capable of generating quizzes on course readings by randomly selecting questions from large pools of similar questions for a given lesson, grading the quizzes, displaying grading results for students who complete quizzes, and mailing these grades to individual LIB 150 professors.[12]

We avoided incorporating online chat sessions into our course because we felt they would unnecessarily fix locations and times for some course activity and would undermine the advantages of asynchronicity, for ourselves and for students.[13] My colleagues and I used an informal, conversational tone in all written instructional materials. This tone coincides well with online culture, and I hope it helps personalize students' experiences and makes them feel at ease as they work through the course.[14] My previous positive experiences with strong Web organizational features, such as presenting standard navigation features on each page, including the URL of each page on the page itself, listing the creation date and the last revised date on each page, and consistently providing information on whom to contact with questions, prompted me to include these features in the LIB 150 Web.[15] I am the primary author of the Web-based materials, but others have contributed material as well. In order to maintain consistency, I act as editor for all written materials.

Throughout development, we took care to make our pages accessible to those with hearing or sight impairments. Images contain explanatory "alt" attributes that can be read using screen-reading software available on a computer in the library. For the streaming audio materials, a text-only alternative is provided.

Expanding our course materials and presenting them in the Web environment has been a challenging, labor-intensive activity. However, this activity has forced us to clarify and focus on the most important skills and concepts we teach and has thereby allowed us to improve the overall content of our instructional materials while, at the same time, improving their presentation. We now have a rather comprehensive and well-integrated set of materials for teaching information literacy. At least for the near future, maintaining and developing these materials will not require the same intensity of effort as did the initial development.

1998 Summer Institute for Faculty Development

For five weeks during the summer of 1998, I participated in the first Summer Institute for Faculty Development, an FLC program designed to provide time and support to faculty working on projects involving the use of technology in teaching. Seven other faculty members from a variety of departments also participated. Each of us had written project proposals that had been deemed worthy of support provided through the Institute, and we were expected to come as close as possible to completing our proposed projects during the five-week program. Our library systems administrator, Allen Greenwood, served as technical coordinator for the Institute, coordinating almost daily seminar sessions attended by all participants, teaching a wide variety of technical skills, and providing access to various technical tools and to server space. During that time, I devoted more than two hundred hours to developing the Web-based self-study course materials for LIB 150. Two of my librarian colleagues, Jeff Frisbie and Elayne Walstedter, also worked more than fifty hours each on this project. It is difficult to determine the amount of time that the library systems administrator devoted to the project because he was also involved in other Institute projects and in coordinating the program at the time, but his involvement was extensive and crucial. He set up the LIB 150 e-mail discussion lists, and developed and programmed the online quiz system. We also hired a student programmer, Casey Paiz, who worked full-time for the Institute's five-week period developing the online calendar utility and assisting with some technical details.

This development experience demonstrated the high value of having access to technical experts, preferably as members of the library staff. Such experts need not have library degrees as long as they are open to working closely with librarians to serve the needs of library users and as long as librarians are open to working closely with them as well. In fact, given the levels at which the library profession seems to pay technical experts, it seems unreasonable to require both a library degree and a technical degree. Overemphasizing the importance of the library degree when hiring technical experts may limit a library's potential to explore cutting-edge technological applications that require in-depth technical knowledge. We could not have reached the level of interactivity currently represented in our online materials without involving technical experts. Because we employ our own technical experts, we are much more assured that we will be able to effectively maintain those interactive course components than we would be had we hired a consultant to develop them. Hiring talented students can be a cost-effective way to extend the reach of permanent systems/programming employees, and it is a wonderful way to provide students with a valuable learning experience.

The Institute also demonstrated the importance of having a reasonable amount of time to concentrate fully on the project when developing an online course. It would have been much more difficult for me to develop the self-study version of LIB 150 had I remained heavily involved in my other library duties throughout the summer.

Involving other librarians in the development process was an important objective of my participation in the Summer Institute. The experience would serve as an important professional development opportunity for the librarians involved who would learn a great deal about creating materials for the Web. Also, from past experience, I know how important it is to involve people in a large library project, particularly a project involving technology, so that others have a sense of ownership (T. Greenwood 1997, 64). This sense of ownership makes people more likely to participate in further project development and also lends enthusiasm to their view of the project when they present it to others. I hope the involvement of other librarians in the development process will continue to lead to increased enthusiasm about the course.

Development Tools and Environment

We used the following tools and environment to develop our online course materials.

   • *Library Web server environment:* Since 1997, Reed Library has employed a library systems administrator. The original systems administrator brought up and maintained the library Web server, and the administrator who succeeded him has continued to maintain and develop it. The server originally ran on a 133 Mhz Pentium computer that had 64 MB of memory (RAM). This computer ran the Red Hat Linux operating system distributed at a cost of approximately fifty dollars. The Apache Web server software came with the Red Hat distribution of Linux, and we used this software for our Web server. The initial investment in getting started with a library Web server was very low. We continue to use the Apache Web server on a machine running the Linux operating system, the only difference being that the server computer has been upgraded considerably. Even the upgrades have been relatively inexpensive when compared with the positive impact on library service accomplished through having our own server.

   • *Quizzes:* The online quiz environment makes use of the library Web server, MSQL database server software (free for educational use),[16] and Java Servlets (usable through an extension to the Apache Web server and supported in most popular Web servers), which provide interactivity between the course Web pages and the database of quiz questions, as well as grading functionality.

•   *E-mail discussion lists:* The section e-mail discussion lists run on Majordomo list software on the library Web server.[17]

•   *Course calendar utility:* The course calendar utility makes use of the library Web server, MSQL database server software, and Java applets contained in Web pages. It contains a student mode for accessing important course information and a teacher mode for creating and editing individual section calendars.

We have found that a library that is willing to be creative in combining and using free and/or inexpensive software for Web development can accomplish a great deal with a small-to-moderate financial investment. However, to take advantage of free software, the library must employ people capable of, and interested in, such experimentation (A. Greenwood 1998).

The Future

We will need to conduct a more formal evaluation of our program. Kaplowitz and Contini (1998, 20) noted that "very little has been done in the area of objectively evaluating CAI in general. Even less has been done in evaluating CAI applications to library instruction" (1998, 20). Conducting evaluations of the computer-assisted instruction related to LIB 150 would certainly aid in future course development and contribute to assessment of the overall college curriculum. The activity could also serve as a model for evaluating other such instructional efforts.

I hope to make FLC faculty increasingly aware of our LIB 150 and other instructional materials available on the Web so they will refer to them as study/research aids for their own assignments. My colleagues and I must continue and expand our efforts to communicate with faculty regarding research education needed at various levels in the curriculum so we can make our own contributions as well as respond to the needs of faculty and students in this area. These communication activities include serving on faculty committees, communicating directly with our liaison department(s), writing to faculty at large, and finding other effective means to involve ourselves in the academic life of the campus.

Conclusions

Academic librarians have long been creative partners in the educational process. It is now time for us to become even more dynamically and directly involved in the teaching process itself. We possess the knowledge others need to pursue lifelong learning in order to thrive in a rapidly changing world, and we can share this knowledge in the classroom. I share a hope with many other librarians that course work in information literacy will become a curricular requirement in an increasing number of programs of higher education. In order to lead our students and our campuses toward curricula that emphasize information literacy, we must step outside our libraries and step up our current efforts to join with faculty and administrators in charting the futures of our institutions. To be as effective and forward looking as possible in this capacity, we must paddle even faster than others in the currents of change, and we must help others see and follow the course ahead.

Notes

1. Information literacy has been defined many times in the recent literature, and the definitions differ only slightly from one another. My own definition is distilled from the many versions I have read and heard in professional presentations as well as from my own teaching: An information-literate person is able to recognize an information need, capable of locating information to respond to a variety of such needs, skilled at evaluating and selecting the best from all information found, and capable of using that information to create new knowledge or to otherwise satisfy an information need.

2. For an in-depth discussion of the history of LIB 150, including the details of the development and administration processes, see T. Greenwood 1998e, "A Traveler's Guide to Exploring Planet Library."

3. RIO is available online from http://dizzy.library.arizona.edu/rio/.

4. The program may have changed since 1995, but I could find no evidence of online materials for the course on the WKU library Web.

5. This assignment is similar to one done by students in the Internet Navigator course in which, for their final projects, students choose their best resources and explain their choices. Internet Navigator students, however, are not provided with evaluation criteria; each student develops his or her own based on individual information needs. Due to time constraints, developing individual criteria would be difficult to accomplish in LIB 150 classes. See Hansen and Lombardo (1997, 72).

6. The fall 1996 term was an exception to the weekly meetings. For this term, each section met twice a week for half the term. One set of LIB 150 sections met for the first seven weeks, and the second set met for the final seven weeks of the term. This schedule was submitted prior to my arrival at FLC. Because many students who registered for an LIB 150 section in the second set forgot to attend the course when it commenced in the middle of the term and because notifying all second-half students about the start of the course would have been difficult and time-consuming, all LIB 150 sections offered after fall 1996 have begun at the start and continued through the end of the term.

7. Vishwanatham, Wilkins, and Jevec note that a solely online teaching environment excludes the possibility for fruitful learning by the less technologically experienced: "Overcoming anxiety and unfamiliarity with computers in general might require a hands-on approach, and in such an online instruction environment it is not possible to reach those individuals who need special attention" (1997, 442).

8. The self-study version of the course retains the science fiction theme. Students choose roles to assume in a new society and view the video produced for the original version of the course.

9. Kaplowitz and Contini (1998, 22) noted no significant differences in student learning of research concepts through computer-aided instruction delivery as opposed to lecture delivery of content.

10. Dewald (1996a, 75) speaks of asynchronicity in relation to computer-mediated communications such as e-mail, but the Web represents a similar asynchronous environment.

11. Kaplowitz and Contini (1998, 26–27) projected that these benefits could be achieved by using the Web rather than a stand-alone computer-aided instruction program for teaching research skills and concepts.

12. Quizzes are accessible from the LIB 150 coursepack contents page (T. Greenwood 1999c).

13. Orr, Appleton, and Andrews (1996, 230) noted that chat was less useful than expected in online instruction.

14. Others have noted the usefulness of the informal approach including Engle (1997, 171) and Dupuis (1998).

15. I did not maintain the dates of creation on the WIU Library Web pages; but, in hindsight, I felt it would have been useful (T. Greenwood 1997, 63–75).

16. Software is available from Hughes Technologies at http://www.hughes.com.au/.

17. Software is available from Great Circle Associates at http://www.greatcircle.com/.

References

About the PLUTO Project. 1995. Available from http://bigdog.lib.purdue.edu/library_info/instruction/tutorials/PLUTO.cgi/pluto/Tutorials/about.html; INTERNET. Link no longer valid.

Alexander, Linda. 1995. LME 101: A required course in basic library skills. *Research Strategies* 13:245–49.

Bender, Laura, and Jeff Rosen. 1998. On the road to teaching information literacy: Worth it, bumps and all. Presentation at LOEX of the West conference, 19 June 1998, at Southern Utah University, Cedar City, Utah.

Clute, John, and Peter Nicholls, eds. 1993. *The Encyclopedia of Science Fiction*. New York: St. Martin's Press.

Daragan, Patricia, and Gwendolyn Stevens. 1996. Developing lifelong learners: An integrative and developmental approach to information literacy. *Research Strategies* 14(2):68–81.

DeLoatch, Karen, and Claire O'Connor. 2000. Capital Community College library and information skills tutorial: The Internet version. 6th ed. [cited February 2001]. Available from http://webster.commnet.edu/libroot/workbook/wrkbk.htm; INTERNET.

Dewald, Nancy H. 1996a. Communicating via computer in library credit courses. *College and Research Libraries News* 57(2):75.

———. 1996b. Computer-mediated communication in library credit courses. *Research Strategies* 14(3):169–76.

Division of Library and Information Services Instruction Group, Plattsburgh State University of New York. 1998. LIB101 spring 1998 schedule. Available from http://www.plattsburgh.edu/acadvp/libinfo/groups/instruct/schds98.html; INTERNET. Link no longer valid.

Division of Library and Information Services Instruction Program Mission

Statement. 1997 [cited 9 July 1997]. Available from http://
www.plattsburgh.edu/acadvp/libinfo/groups/instruct/nyla/Instmis.htm;
INTERNET. Link no longer valid.

Dupuis, Elizabeth. 1998. Keynote address. LOEX of the West conference, 19 June
1998, at Southern Utah University, Cedar City, Utah.

Engle, Michael O. 1997. Instruction and the Web: The development of a library
research tutorial. In *The Library Web*, ed. Julie M. Still. Medford, N.J.:
Information Today.

Ercegovac, Zorana. 1995. Information access instruction (IAI⁴): Design principles.
College and Research Libraries 56(3):249–57.

Greenwood, Allen. 1997. John F. Reed Library main Web page. Available from
http://library.fortlewis.edu/; INTERNET.

———— . 1998. Conversation with author, Durango, Colo., 30 August 1998.

Greenwood, Tina Evans. 1997. The Western Illinois University Library World
Wide Web home page. In *The Library Web*, ed. Julie M. Still. Medford, N.J.:
Information Today.

———— . 1998a. Evaluating nonprint sources — A guide to writing your nonprint
source evaluations for assignment 4 [cited 27 July 1998]. Available from
http://library.fortlewis.edu/~instruct/lib150/nonprinteval.html; INTERNET.

———— . 1998b. Evaluating your learning experience, essay questions [cited 2 July
1998]. Available from http://library.fortlewis.edu/~instruct/lib150/essay.html;
INTERNET.

———— . 1998c. Personal interest and experience questionnaire [cited 15 June
1998]. Available from http://library.fortlewis.edu/~instruct/lib150/
question.html; INTERNET.

———— . 1998d. Topic selection advice sheet [cited 7 July 1998]. Available from
http://library.fortlewis.edu/~instruct/lib150/advice.html; INTERNET. Link
no longer valid.

———— . 1998e. A traveler's guide to exploring planet library—Information
literacy at Fort Lewis College. *Colorado Libraries* 24(4):12–16.

———— . 1999a. Assignment 4: Locating information in nonprint sources [cited 19
August 1999]. Available from http://library.fortlewis.edu/~instruct/lib150/
assign4.html; INTERNET. Link no longer valid.

———— . 1999b. Evaluating book sources — A guide to writing your book source
evaluations for assignment 2 [cited 18 August 1999]. Available from http://
library.fortlewis.edu/~instruct/lib150/bookeval.html; INTERNET.

———— . 1999c. A traveler's guide to exploring planet library or coursepack for
LIB 150, information literacy [cited 19 November 1999]. Available from
http://library.fortlewis.edu/~instruct/lib150/contents.html; INTERNET.

———— . 2000. Final bibliography project [cited 11 April 2000]. Available from
http://library.fortlewis.edu/~instruct/lib150/final.html; INTERNET.

Greenwood, Tina Evans, and Jeff Frisbie. 1999. Evaluating periodical sources—A
guide to writing your periodical source evaluations for assignment 3 [cited 17
March 1999]. Available from http://library.fortlewis.edu/~instruct/lib150/
perdeval.html; INTERNET. Link no longer valid.

Hansen, Carol, and Nancy Lombardo. 1997. Toward the virtual university:
Collaborative development of a Web-based course. *Research Strategies*
15(2):68–79.

Internet Navigator course. 1996. Available from http://www-navigator.utah.edu/;
INTERNET.

Internet Navigator student information. 1998 [cited 11 June 1998]. Available from http://medstat.med.utah.edu/navigator/intro/students.html; INTERNET. Link no longer valid.

Jayne, Elaine, and Patricia Vander Meer. 1997. The library's role in academic instructional use of the World Wide Web. *Research Strategies* 15(3):123–50.

Jenkins, Althea H., Laverne Simoneaux, and William Miller. 1998. Provosts, libraries and electronic information: Reports from AAHE and CNI. *College and Research Libraries News* 59(6):420–21.

Jones, Debra. 1996. Information research [cited 20 September 1996]. Available from http://libwww.cabrillo.cc.ca.us/html/about/l10/l10obj.html; INTERNET.

Kaplowitz, Joan, and Janice Contini. 1998. Computer-assisted instruction: Is it an option for bibliographic instruction in large undergraduate survey classes? *College and Research Libraries* 59(1):19–27.

Library skills programs at U of A: Background/plans. 1996. Available from http://dizzy.library.arizona.edu/infolit/LSP.HTM; INTERNET.

List, Carla. 1995. Branching out: A required library research course targets disciplines and programs. *Reference Librarian* (51–52):385–98.

Malone, Debbie, and Carol Videon. 1997. Assessing undergraduate use of electronic resources: A quantitative analysis of works cited. *Research Strategies* 15(3):151–58.

Orr, Debbie, Margaret Appleton, and Trish Andrews. 1996. Teaching information literacy skills to remote students through an interactive workshop. *Research Strategies* 14(4):224–33.

PLUTO. 1995. Available from http://bigdog.lib.purdue.edu/library_info/instruction/tutorials/PLUTO.cgi/pluto/Tutorials/pmenu1.html?1574239489; INTERNET. Link no longer valid.

PLUTO quiz introduction. 1995. Available from http://bigdog.lib.purdue.edu/library_info/instruction/tutorials/PLUTO.cgi/pluto/Tutorials/quiz.html?1574239489; INTERNET. Link no longer valid.

Smalley, Topsy N. 18 July 1998. Our information research course [Internet, e-mail to the author]. Available as e-mail from the author (greenwood_t@fortlewis.edu).

Stamatoplos, Anthony, and Robert Mackoy. 1998. Effects of library instruction on university students' satisfaction with the library: A longitudinal study. *College and Research Libraries* 59(4):323–34.

Vishwanatham, Rama, Walter Wilkins, and Thomas Jevec. 1997. The Internet as a medium for online instruction. *College and Research Libraries* 58(5):433–44.

West, Sharon M., and Diane Ruess. 1995. The electronic library: Teaching students at a distance. In *The Impact of Technology on Library Instruction: Papers and Session Materials Presented at the Twenty-first National LOEX Library Instruction Conference Held in Racine, Wisconsin 14 to 15 May 1993*, ed. Linda Shirato. Ann Arbor, Mich.: Pierian Press.

When Worlds Collide. 1951. Directed by Rudolph Maté. 81 min. Paramount Home Video. Videocassette.

Wyle, Philip, and Edwin Balmer. 1933. *When Worlds Collide.* New York: Dell.

About the Authors

Elizabeth A. Dupuis is currently Head of the Digital Information Literacy Office at the University of Texas at Austin, responsible for managing the instructional services of the General Libraries. She earned her MLS from the University of Illinois at Urbana-Champaign. She can be reached at beth@mail.utexas.edu.

Arglenda Friday (MLS, University of Maryland, 1974) has years of experience in special (law/medical), academic, and public libraries. She has held various positions including tenured faculty and Library Diversity Coordinator at San Jose State University, and is presently the Executive Director of the African-American Research Library and Cultural Center, Broward County Libraries Division. She can be reached via e-mail at fridaya@hotmail.com.

Kathryn Graves has been a reference librarian/bibliographer at the University of Kansas since 1988. She is currently the Reference Coordinator at KU's Watson Library. She earned her MLS from the University of South Carolina. She can be reached at kgraves@ku.edu.

Tina Evans Greenwood is a native of Arizona and currently resides in Durango, Colorado, where she is Library Instruction Coordinator at Fort Lewis College. She earned undergraduate degrees in English and history from the University of Arizona, a master's degree in Latin American Studies from Tulane University and a master's in library science from the University of Arizona. She has published work in the areas of Latin American history and library instruction. She has also presented on her work in information literacy at state and national conferences, and she has been a participant in the Library Leadership Institute at Snowbird and the Institute for Information Literacy. She is currently very active in campus and library governance at Fort Lewis College. Contact information: phone: 970-247-7684; e-mail: greenwood_t@fortlewis.edu; Web: http://library.fortlewis.edu/~instruct/tina/web/resume.html.

Kelly M. Jordan is currently the Information Technology/Engineering Reference Liaison Librarian at George Mason University in Fairfax, Virginia. She can be reached at kjordan2@gmu.edu.

Maurie Caitlin Kelly received her BA in History from the Pennsylvania State University and her MSLS from Clarion University of Pennsylvania. She has worked with government information for over ten years at the University of Illinois at Chicago, Penn State University, and now as the State GIS Librarian and Coordinator for the official geospatial data clearinghouse for the Commonwealth of Pennsylvania (PASDA—www.pasda.psu.edu). She has worked and written often on student retention issues. Maurie can be reached at mck4@psu.edu.

Andrea Kross received her MLIS degree in 1993 from Dalhousie University in Halifax, Nova Scotia. Prior to this, she earned her BSc (Zoology major), BA Honors in Linguistics, and MSc in Psycholinguistics degrees from the University of Alberta. As part of her NSERC Scholarship in Science Librarianship, Andrea completed two summer internships, one in the cataloging department of the Canada Institute for Scientific and Technical Information (CISTI), and the other at the W.K. Kellogg Health Sciences Library at Dalhousie University. For five years, she worked at the Captain John Smith Library at Christopher Newport University, where she was the Assistant Catalog/Reference Librarian until she was promoted to Catalog Librarian.

In 2001, Andrea left Virginia to work for Innovative Interfaces, Inc., where she is an Implementation Consultant. She currently lives in Concord, California, and can be contacted at andikross@yahoo.com.

Stephanie Michel received her MLS degree from Indiana University in 1997. For three years, she served as a Reference/Instruction Librarian at Radford University in Virginia. **Caroline Gibson** also received her MLS from Indiana University in 1997 and was a Reference/Instruction Librarian at Radford. While at Radford University, the authors collaborated on the activities discussed in their chapter. Currently, Stephanie Michel is a Humanities Reference Librarian at the University of Oregon, Eugene Oregon, and can be reached at smichel@oregon.uoregon.edu. Caroline Gilson is a Reference Librarian at the Evansville Vanderburgh Co. Public Library, Evansville Indiana, and can be reached at caroline@evcpl.lib.in.us.

Cindy Pierard is the Instruction Coordinator at the University of Kansas Libraries. She has a B.A. in International Studies from Earlham College and an M.L.S. from Indiana University. In addition to student outreach programs, her interests include collaboration and assessment. Her e-mail address is cpierard@ku.edu.

Deborah Poole, MLIS, is Coordinator for Public Services, Associate Professor, J. Edgar and Louise S. Monroe Library, New Orleans.

Darla Rushing began her career in librarianship as a student worker in her undergraduate college, never conceiving that the experience would lead to a life-time commitment to the profession. With undergraduate degrees in history and music and the MLS from Louisiana State University, she has previously held positions in music cataloging and museum librarianship. She is currently Coordinator for Technical Services at Loyola University New Orleans. She has written in the areas of music bibliography and technical services management.